ARTIFICIAL INTELLIGENCE

A Theoretical Guide

By Mohit Thakkar

About the Book:

It often happens that when we try to study a subject for some examination or a job interview, we just don't find the right content.

The problem with the reference books is that they are too descriptive for last moment studies. Whereas the problem with local publications is that they are inaccurate as compared to the reference books.

This particular book encapsulates the subject notes on *Artificial Intelligence* with the combined benefits of reference books & local publications. It has the accuracy of a reference book as well as the abstraction of a local publication.

The author studied the subject from various sources such as web lectures, reference books, online tutorials & so on. After having a thorough understanding of the subject, the author compiled this book for an easy understanding of the subject.

This book presents the content with utmost simplicity of language, and in an abstract manner so that it can be used for last moment studies. This book can be used by:

- Students to prepare for their examinations
- Professionals to prepare for job interviews.
- Individuals willing to have a basic understanding of the domain: *Artificial Intelligence*.

Happy Reading!

References:

1. Artificial Intelligence - Elaine Rich, Kevin Knight & Shivashankar Nair - (3rd Edition), Tata McGraw-Hill

2. PROLOG Programming for Artificial Intelligence - Ivan Bratko – Addison Wesley Publishing Company

Disclaimer:

The content in this book is compiled from various sources & also contains personal views of the author. Some of the content in this book might be inherited from other books. The author claims no rights to such content. The rights to any such content remains with the respective owners (mentioned in the References).

© 2018 Mohit Thakkar

All rights reserved. No part of this publication may be reproduced, stored in a retrieval system, or transmitted in any form or by any means, electronic, mechanical, photocopying, recording, or otherwise, without prior written permission of the publisher.

Contents:

- **Chapter 1: What is Artificial Intelligence?** 1
    - Introduction to Artificial Intelligence 2
    - Acting Humanly: The Turing Test Approach 3
    - The State of the Art (AI Applications) 5
    - Classification of AI 6
    - The AI Problems 7
    - The Underlying Assumptions about AI 8
    - What is an AI Technique? 9
    - Criteria for Success (Turing Test) 10

- **Chapter 2: Problems, Problem Spaces & Heuristic Search Techniques** 11
    - Agents & Environment 12
    - Defining the Problem as a State Space Search 14
        - Play Chess Problem 16
        - Water Jug Problem 17
        - 8 Puzzle Problem 19
        - Tower of Hanoi Problem 21
        - Travelling Salesman Problem 22
        - 8-Queen Problem 24
        - Missionaries & Cannibals Problem 25
        - Monkey & Banana Problem 28
        - Cryptarithmetic Problem 29
        - Blocks World Problem 31
        - Tic-Tac-Toe (Xs & Os) Problem 32
    - AI Problem Characteristics 33
    - Production System 39
    - Issues in the Design of Search Programs 40
    - Control Strategies 41
    - Brute-Force / Undirected Search Control Strategy 42
        - Breadth-First Search 42
        - Depth-First Search 45
        - Breadth-First Search versus Depth-First Search 47
    - Heuristic / Directed Search Control Strategy 48
        - Generate-And-Test 48
        - Hill Climbing 49

- Simple Hill Climbing 49
- Steepest-Ascent Hill Climbing 50
- Issues in Hill Climbing 51
- Simulated Annealing 53
- Hill Climbing versus Simulated Annealing 55
- Best-First Search 56
    - A* Algorithm 58
- Problem Reduction 63
    - AO* Algorithm 64
- Constraint Satisfaction 66
- Means-Ends Analysis 68
  - Examples: Cryptarithmetic Problems 69

> **Chapter 3: Knowledge Representation Issues** 77

  - Representations & Mappings 78
  - Approaches to Knowledge Representation 80
  - Declarative versus Procedural Representation of Knowledge 82
  - Issues in Knowledge Representation 83
  - The Frame Problem 85
  - Expert System 86
    - Knowledge Acquisition 87
    - Expert System Shell 88

> **Chapter 4: Using Predicate Logic** 89

  - Introduction to Logic 90
  - Representing Simple Facts in Logic 91
  - Representing Instance & ISA Relationships 93
  - Computable Functions & Predicates 95
  - Resolution 96
    - Conversion to Clause Form 97
    - Propositional Resolution 99
    - The Unification Algorithm 100
    - Predicate Logic Resolution 102
  - Examples 103

> **Chapter 5: Representing Knowledge Using Rules** 115

- o Procedural versus Declarative Knowledge 116
- o Logic Programming 117
- o Forward versus Backward Reasoning 118
- o PROLOG uses Backward Chaining 120
- o Conflict Resolution in Rule-Based System 122

- ➢ **Chapter 6: Symbolic Reasoning Under Uncertainty** 125
  - o Introduction to Reasoning 126
  - o Introduction to Non-Monotonic Reasoning 127
  - o Logics for Non-Monotonic Reasoning 128
    - Default Reasoning 128
      - Non-Monotonic Logic 128
      - Default Logic 128
    - Methods of Logical Reasoning 130
      - Deduction 130
      - Induction 131
      - Abduction 132

- ➢ **Chapter 7: Statistical Reasoning** 133
  - o Introduction to Statistical Reasoning 134
  - o Probability & Bays' Theorem 135
  - o Certainty Factors & Rule-Based Systems 137
  - o Bayesian Networks 139
  - o Dempster-Shafer Theory 141
  - o Fuzzy Logic 143

- ➢ **Chapter 8: Slot-and-Filler Structures** 145
  - o Semantic Nets 146
  - o Frames 151

- ➢ **Chapter 9: Game Playing & Planning** 153
  - o Game Playing 154

- Overview 154
- Min-Max Search Procedure 156
- Alpha-beta Pruning 160
- Examples 163

o Planning 169
- An Example Domain – The Blocks World 169
- Components of a Planning System 171
- Goal Stack Planning 172

➢ **Chapter 10: Natural Language Processing** 175

o Introduction to Natural Language Processing 176
o Syntactic Processing 179
o Semantic Analysis 181
o Discourse & Pragmatic Processing 182

➢ **Chapter 11: Connectionist Models** 185

o Introduction: Hopfield Networks 186
o Artificial Neural Networks 189
o Activation Functions 191
o Application of Neural Networks 193
o Learning in Neural Networks 194
- Perceptron 194
- Perceptron Learning Algorithm 196
- Linear Separability 197
- Supervised and Unsupervised Learning 199
o Connectionist AI & Symbolic AI 200

➢ **Chapter 12: Introduction to PROLOG** 201

o Introduction to Prolog: Facts, Objects & Variables 202
o Conjunctions in Prolog (Backward Chaining) 204
o List Manipulation in Prolog 206
- Membership in a List 207
- Concatenation of Lists 208
- Adding & Deleting from a List 210

- ▪ Sub-List 212

- o **Cut, Fail & Repeat Predicates in Prolog** 213
  - ▪ Cut 213
  - ▪ Fail 215
  - ▪ Repeat 216

- o Terminologies in Prolog 217
- o Prolog Programs 219

List of Figures:

- Figure 1.1: Turing Test 3
- Figure 1.2: Turing Test 10
- Figure 2.1: Agents & Environment 12
- Figure 2.2: 8 Puzzle Problem 19
- Figure 2.3: 8 Puzzle Problem – Solution Search Tree 20
- Figure 2.4: Tower of Hanoi Problem – Solution Search Tree 21
- Figure 2.5: Travelling Salesman Problem 22
- Figure 2.6: Travelling Salesman Problem – Solution Search Tree 23
- Figure 2.7: 8-Queen Problem - Goal State 24
- Figure 2.8: Missionaries & Cannibals Problem 25
- Figure 2.9: Missionaries & Cannibals Problem - Solution Search Tree 27
- Figure 2.10: The Monkey & Banana Problem 28
- Figure 2.11: Cryptarithmetic Puzzle – Search Tree 30
- Figure 2.12: Blocks World Problem 31
- Figure 2.13: Tic-Tac-Toe (Xs & Os) Problem 32
- Figure 2.14: Breadth-First Search Tree 42
- Figure 2.15: Depth-First Search Tree 45
- Figure 2.16: Issues in Hill Climbing 51
- Figure 2.17: 8-Puzzle Problem - A* Algorithm – Example 1 60
- Figure 2.18: 8-Puzzle Problem - A* Algorithm – Example 2 62
- Figure 2.19: AND-OR Graph 63
- Figure 3.1: Mapping between Facts & Representations 78
- Figure 3.2: Representation of Facts 79
- Figure 3.3: Inheritable Knowledge Representation 81
- Figure 3.4: Components of an Expert System 86
- Figure 4.1: Three Ways of Representing Class Membership 93
- Figure 5.1: Forward versus Backward Reasoning 116
- Figure 7.1: Bayesian Network 136
- Figure 7.2: Priority Table for Bayesian Network 137
- Figure 7.3: Conventional (Crisp) versus Fuzzy Logic 140
- Figure 8.1: Semantic Network (Example) 143
- Figure 8.2: Partitioned Semantic Network (Example 1) 145
- Figure 8.3: Partitioned Semantic Network (Example 2) 145
- Figure 8.4: Partitioned Semantic Network (Example 3) 146
- Figure 8.5: Partitioned Semantic Network (Example 4) 146
- Figure 8.6: Partitioned Semantic Network (Example 5) 147
- Figure 8.7: Frames as Set & Instance (Example) 149
- Figure 9.1: One-Ply Min-Max Search 153

- Figure 9.2: Two-Ply Min-Max Search 154
- Figure 9.3: Two-Ply Min-Max Search (Backing-Up the Values) 154
- Figure 9.4: Min-Max Search with Alpha-Beta Pruning 159
- Figure 9.5: Min-Max Search (Example 1) 160
- Figure 9.6: Min-Max Search (Example 1) (Solution) 161
- Figure 9.7: Min-Max Search (Example 2) 162
- Figure 9.8: Min-Max Search (Example 2) (Solution) 163
- Figure 9.9: Min-Max Search (Example 3) 164
- Figure 9.10: Min-Max Search (Example 3) (Ideal Solution) 164
- Figure 9.11: Min-Max Search (Example 3) (Flawed Solution) 165
- Figure 9.12: Goal Stack Planning (Blocks World) 169
- Figure 10.1: Syntactic Analysis – Natural Language Processing (Example 1) 173
- Figure 10.2: Syntactic Analysis – Natural Language Processing (Example 2) .. 176
- Figure 11.1: A Simple Hopfield Network 182
- Figure 11.2: Stable States of a Particular Hopfield Network 183
- Figure 11.3: A Biological Neuron 184
- Figure 11.4: An Artificial Neuron 185
- Figure 11.5: Threshold Activation Function 186
- Figure 11.6: Linear Activation Function 187
- Figure 11.7: Sigmoid Activation Function 187
- Figure 11.8: Perceptron 189
- Figure 11.9: Learning in a Neural Network 190
- Figure 11.10: Linearly Separable Problem 192
- Figure 11.11: Linearly Inseparable Problem 193
- Figure 12.1: List Concatenation in Prolog 204
- Figure 12.2: Membership & Sublist in Prolog Lists 207

What is Artificial Intelligence?

1.1 Introduction to Artificial Intelligence:

Artificial Intelligence (AI) can be defined as a science of making a machine think & act as intelligently (smartly) as a human being.

It is also defined as a branch of computer science that studies and develops intelligent machines and software.

AI can be viewed from a variety of perspectives. Following are the ***four approaches*** to AI that are widely followed:

Thinking Humanly   Thinking Rationally

Acting Humanly   Acting Rationally

The ***approaches on top*** are concerned with ***thought processes & reasoning***, whereas the ***ones on the bottom*** address ***behavior***.

The ***approaches on the left*** measure success in terms of similarity to ***human performance***, whereas the ***ones on the right*** measure success against an ***ideal performance*** measure, called ***rationality***.

A ***system is rational*** if it does the "***right thing***", given what it knows.

AI programs work on ***symbols rather than integers***. The most common ***programming languages*** used to develop ***AI programs*** are ***LISP (List Programming) & PROLOG (PROgramming in LOGic)***.

> ***Fun Fact:*** The feeling of intelligence is a mirage, if you achieve it, it ceases to make you feel so. As somebody has competently put it – AI is Artificial Intelligence until it is achieved, after that the acronym reduces to Already Implemented.

1.2 Acting Humanly: The Turing Test Approach

The **Turing Test**, proposed by **Alan Turing (1950)**, was designed to provide a satisfactory operational definition of **Artificial Intelligence**. An AI computer passes the test if a human interrogator, after posing some written questions, cannot tell whether the written responses come from a person or from a computer.

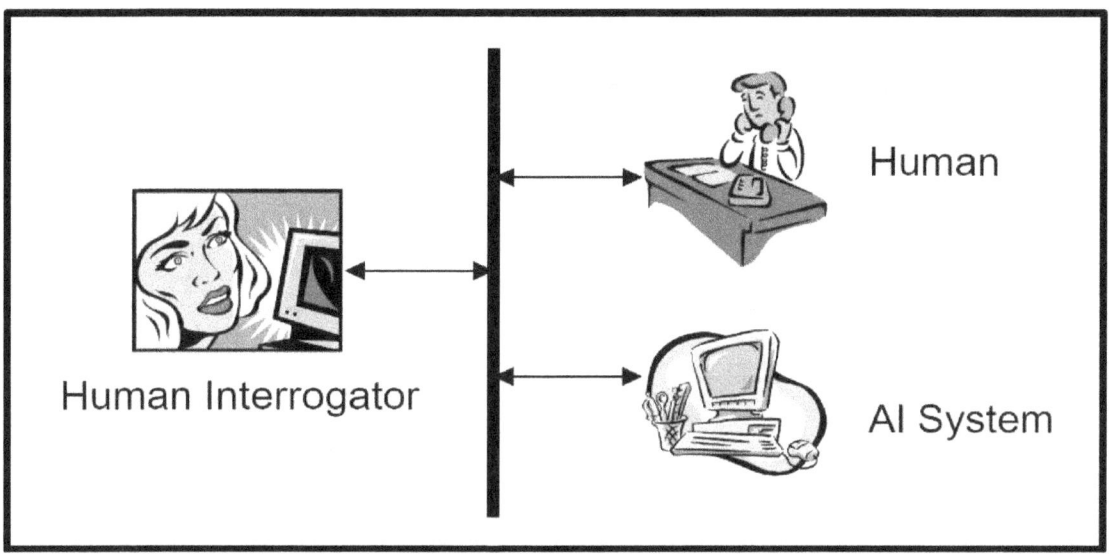

Figure 1.1: Turing Test

For a computer to pass a rigorously applied **Turing Test**, it would need to possess the following capabilities:

- **Natural language processing** to enable it to communicate successfully in English.
- **Knowledge representation** to store what it knows or hears.
- **Automated reasoning** to use the stored information to answer questions & to draw new conclusions.
- **Machine learning** to adapt to new circumstances by detecting & understanding patterns.

Turing's test deliberately avoided direct physical interaction between the interrogator and the computer, because **physical simulation of a person is unnecessary for intelligence**.

However, the **Total Turing Test** includes a **video signal** so that the interrogator can test the **subject's perceptual abilities**. To pass the **Total Turing Test**, the computer will need to possess the following additional capabilities:

- **Computer vision** to perceive objects.

- **Robotics** to manipulate objects and move about.

These six capabilities compose most of **Artificial Intelligence**.

1.3 The State of the Art (AI Applications):

What can AI do today? Here are the few applications:

- **Robotic Vehicles**: A driverless robotic car named STANLEY sped through the rough terrain of the Mojave Desert at 22 mph, finishing the 132-mile course first to win the 2005 DARPA Grand Challenge.

- **Speech Recognition**: A traveler calling Indian Airlines to book a flight can have the entire conversation guided by an automated speech recognition system.

- **Handwriting Recognition**: The handwriting recognition software reads the text written on paper by a pen or on screen by a stylus. It can recognize the shapes of the letters and convert it into editable text.

- **Game Playing**: IBM's DEEP BLUE became the first computer program to defeat the world champion in a chess match by a score of 3.5 to 2.5 in a match.

- **Spam fighting**: Everyday, AI algorithms classify over a billion messages as spam, saving the recipient from having to waste time deleting those messages.

- **Logistics planning**: During the Persian Gulf crisis of 1991, U.S. forces deployed a Dynamic Analysis and Re-planning Tool, DART, to do automated logistics planning and scheduling for transportation. The AI planning techniques generated a plan in hours that would have taken weeks with older methods.

- **Robotics**: The iRobot Corporation has sold over two million robotic vacuum cleaners for home use. The company also deploys the more rugged Robots to Iraq and Afghanistan, where they are used to handle hazardous materials, clear explosives, and identify the location of snipers.

- **Machine Translation**: A computer program automatically translates from one language to another.

- **Data Mining**: Intelligent computer programs can be used to evaluate patterns & mine interesting knowledge from data archives.

- **Enhance Electronic Gadgets**: AI can be used to implement features like face recognition & auto focus in a camera.

1.4 Classification of AI:

Three major types of AI:

- **Weak AI**: The study and design of machines that perform intelligent tasks. Not concerned with how tasks are performed, mostly concerned with performance and logic. E.g., to make a flying machine, use logic and physics, don't mimic a bird.

- **Strong AI**: The study and design of machines that simulate the human mind to perform intelligent tasks. Borrows many ideas from psychology, neuroscience, etc. The goal is to perform tasks the way a human might do them, but implement it on the computer.

- **Emergent AI**: The study and design of machines that simulate simple creatures, and attempt to evolve & have higher level of emergent behavior.

1.5 The AI Problems:

As AI research progressed & techniques for handling larger amounts of knowledge were developed, some developments were made on the existing tasks & new tasks were attempted. The **problems encountered** while attempting the new tasks included:

- *Perception (vision and speech)*
- *Natural language understanding*

Perception of the world around us is crucial to our survival. Animals with much less intelligence than humans are capable of better visual perception than current machines. Perception tasks are difficult for machines because these tasks involve analog signals that are typically very noisy. Also, a large number of things must be perceived at once for visual perception.

The ability to use language to communicate a wide variety of ideas is perhaps the most important thing that separates humans from the other animals. The problem of understanding spoken language is a perceptual problem for a machine & is hard to solve. But suppose we simplify the problem by restricting it to written language. This problem, usually referred to as **Natural Language Understanding**, is still extremely complicated. In order to understand sentences about a topic, it is necessary not only to know a lot about the language itself but also a good deal about the topic so that unstated assumptions can be recognized.

Before studying specific AI problems and solution techniques, it is important to discuss the following four questions:

1. What are our underlying assumptions about intelligence?
2. What kinds of techniques will be useful for solving AI problems?
3. At what level of detail are we trying to model human intelligence?
4. How will we know when we have succeeded in building an intelligent program?

The following sections of this chapter addresses these questions.

1.6 The Underlying Assumptions about AI:

At the heart of AI research lies the **Physical Symbol System Hypothesis (PSSH)**.

A **Physical Symbol System (PSS)** consists of a set of entities, called **Symbols**, which are physical patterns that can occur as components of another type of entity called an **Expression (or symbol structure)**. Thus, an **Expression** is composed of a number of instances of symbols related in some physical way. At any instant of time the system will contain a collection of these symbol structures. Besides these structures, the system also contains a **collection of processes that operate on expressions** to produce other expressions. A **Physical Symbol System** is a machine that produces an evolving collection of symbol structures.

The **Physical Symbol System Hypothesis (PSSH):** A physical symbol system has the necessary and sufficient means for intelligent action.

This hypothesis is only a hypothesis. There appears to be no way to prove or disprove it on logical grounds.

1.7 What is an AI Technique?

Artificial intelligence problems span a very broad spectrum. Techniques that are appropriate for solving a variety of these problems are known as **AI techniques**. Before we begin to examine the individual techniques, let us take a look at the properties they ought to possess.

Artificial Intelligence requires Knowledge & knowledge possesses less desirable properties such as:

- *Voluminous*
- *Hard to characterize accurately*
- *Constantly changing*
- *Differs from data that can be used*

AI technique is a method that deals with the representation of knowledge in such a way that:

- **Knowledge Captures Generalization**: situations that share important properties are grouped together. If knowledge does not have this property, excessive amount of memory and updating will be required. So, we usually state something without this property as "data" rather than knowledge

- **It can be understood by people who must provide it**: most of the knowledge an AI program has, must ultimately be provided by people in terms they understand.

- **It can be easily modified to correct errors**

- **It can be used in variety of situations**

- **It can be used to reduce its own volume by narrowing range of possibilities**

1.8 Criteria for Success (Turing Test):

One of the most important questions to answer in any scientific or engineering research project is "How will we know if we have succeeded?" Artificial intelligence is no exception. *How will we know if we have constructed a machine that is intelligent?*

In *1950*, *Alan Turing* proposed a method, known as *Turing Test*, for determining whether a machine can think. To conduct this test, we need *two people & the machine* to be evaluated. One person plays the role of the *interrogator*, who is in a separate room from *the computer & the other person*.

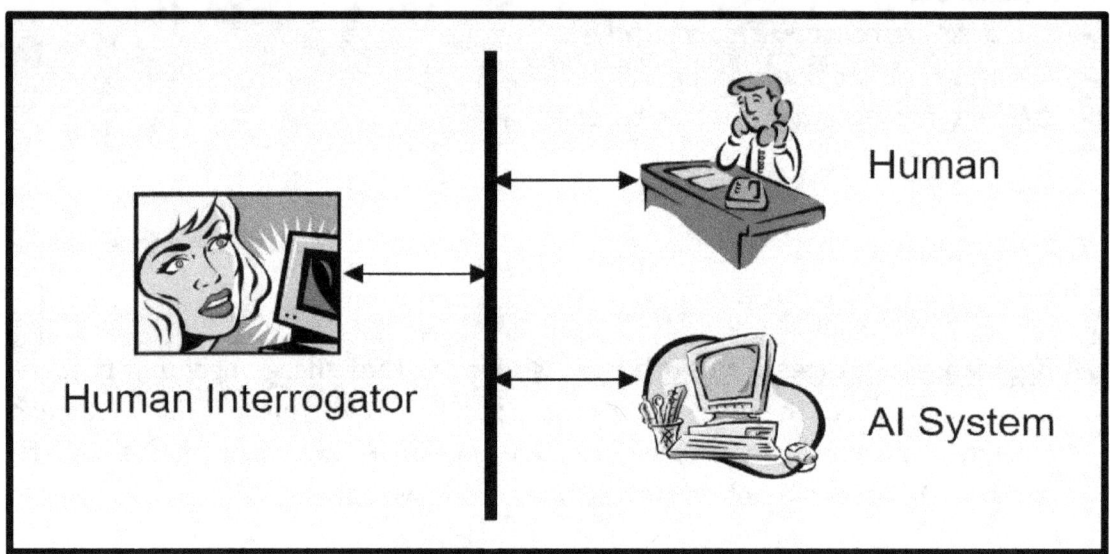

Figure 1.2: Turing Test

The interrogator can ask questions either to the person or to the computer by typing questions and receiving typed responses. However, the interrogator knows them only as A & B and aims to determine which is the person & which is the machine. The goal of the machine is to fool the interrogator into believing that it is the person. if the machine succeeds at this, then we will conclude that the machine can think.

In this way, we will know if we have constructed a machine that's intelligent enough.

Problems, Problem Spaces & Heuristic Search Techniques

2.1 Agents & Environment:

To understand the concept of AI problems, it is necessary to learn about the agents, environments, & the coupling between them.

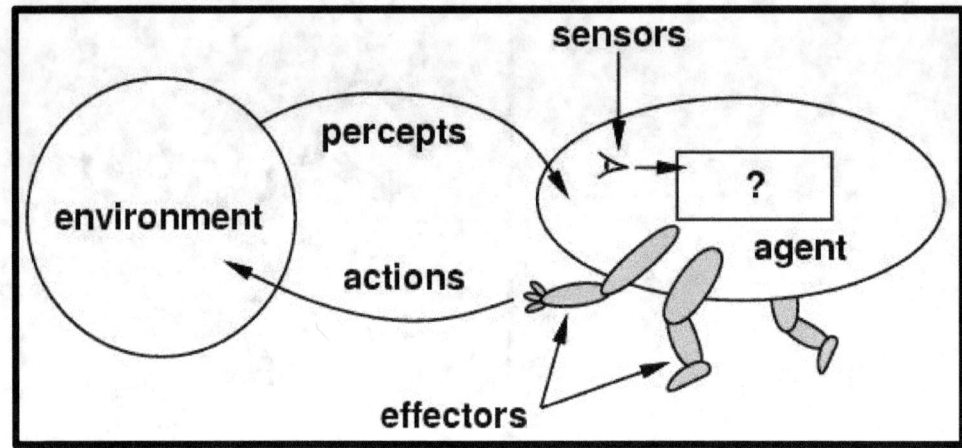

Figure 2.1: Agents & Environment

An *agent* is anything that can be viewed as perceiving its environment through *sensors* & acting upon that environment through *actuators or effectors*.

- *Human Agent*:
  Sensors: Eyes, ears, and other organs.
  Actuators: Hands, legs, vocal tract, and so on.

- *Robotic Agent*:
  Sensors: Cameras & infrared range finders.
  Actuators: Various motors.

- *Software Agent*:
  Sensors: Keystrokes, file contents, & network packets.
  Actuators: Displaying on the screen, writing files, & sending network packets.

The term *percept* refers to the agent's perceptual inputs at any given instant. An agent's *percept sequence* is the complete history of everything the agent has ever perceived. An agent's choice of action at any given instant can depend on the entire percept sequence observed till date.

An *agent* should be able to sense & act. But an *intelligent agent* should have the following capabilities:

1. *Sense.*
2. *Act.*
3. *Understand, Reason & Learn.*
4. *Autonomous up to certain extent.*
5. *Rational*

A **rational agent** is one that does the right thing. Rationality refers to a good sense of reasoning. The ability of the agent to take rational decision depends on the following four parameters:

1. Performance Measure (Criteria for success).
2. Agent's prior knowledge of the environment.
3. Actions that the agent can carry out.
4. Agent's percept sequence till date.

A **rational agent** will always select an **action based on the percept sequence** it has received so far as to **maximize the performance measure**.

2.2 Defining the Problem as a State Space Search:

Problem solving is the major area of concern in **Artificial Intelligence**. To solve a particular problem, we need to build a **system which can generate required solution**.

Suppose we start with the problem statement **"Play chess"**. For a machine, this is a **very incomplete statement of the problem** we want to solve. To build a program that could "Play chess", we would first have to **specify the starting position** of the chess board, **the rules that define the legal moves**, & **the board positions that represent a win** for one side or the other.

For the problem **"Play chess"**, it is fairly easy to provide a formal and complete **problem description**. The **starting position** can be described as an **8 x 8 array** where each position contains a symbol for the appropriate piece in the official chess opening position. We can **define our goal** as **any board position in which the opponent does not have a legal move & his or her king is under attack**. The **legal moves** provide the way of getting from **the initial state to a goal state**. They can be described easily as a **set of rules**.

However, if we **write such rules individually**, we have to write a **very large number of them** since there has to be a separate rule for each of the roughly 10^{120} **possible board positions**. Using so many rules poses two serious practical difficulties:

> *No person could ever supply a complete set of such rules. It would take too long and could certainly not be done without mistakes.*

> *No program could easily handle all those rules.*

In order to minimize such problems, we should look for a way to write the **rules describing the legal moves in as general a way as possible**. It can be done by describing a problem as a **State Space Search**. Consider the following:

Defining the Problem & Search:

A **Problem** is described formally as the combination of the following:

- **State Space**: Define a **state space** that contains all the **possible configurations of relevant objects**. **For example**, all the possible board positions in a Chess game.

- **Initial State**: Specify one or more states within the state space from which the problem-solving process may start. These states are called **initial states**. **For example**, starting position of the board in a Chess game.

- **Goal State**: Specify one or more states that would be acceptable as **solutions to the problem**. These states are called **goal states**. **For example**, the board positions that represent a win in a chess game.

- **Set of Rules**: Specify a set of rules that describe the actions available. **For example**, the valid moves in a chess game.

The problem can then be solved by using the rules, in combination with an appropriate strategy, to move through the problem space until a path from an initial state to a goal state is found. This process is known as **Search**.

Defining the State & State Space:

A **State** is a **representation of the problem elements** (32 pieces in a chess game) at a given moment.

A **State Space** is the **set of all states reachable from the initial state**.

A **State Space** forms a **graph** in which the **nodes are the states** and the **edges between the nodes are the actions**. In state space, a **path** is a sequence of **states connected by a sequence of actions**.

The **state space representation** forms the **basis of most of the AI methods**. In the following section of the chapter, we will study the **State Space Search representation** of some of the **common problems**.

2.2.1 Play Chess Problem:

To build a program that could play chess, we have to specify:

> ➤ The **starting position** of the chess board.
> ➤ The **rules** that define legal moves.
> ➤ The **board position that represents a win**.

The starting position can be described by an 8 X 8 array:

$$\text{square } (x, y)$$
x varying from 1 to 8
y varying from 1 to 8

in which each element describes the board position of an appropriate piece in the official chess opening position.

The goal is any board position in which the **opponent does not have a legal move & his or her "king" is under attack**.

The legal moves provide the way of getting from initial state of final state. It can be described as a **set of rules** consisting of **two parts**: **A left side** that gives the **current position** & **the right side** that describes the **new board position after the legal move**.

Example:

While pawn at Square (5, 2) AND Square (5, 3) is empty AND Square (5, 4) is empty
Move pawn from Square (5, 2) to Square (5, 4)

The **current position** of a chess coin on the board is its **state** and the **set of all possible states** is **state space**. One or more **states where the problem terminates** are **goal states**.

Chess has approximately 10^{120} **game paths**. These positions comprise the problem **search space**. Using above formulation, the **problem of playing chess** is defined as a **problem of moving around in a state space**, where each state corresponds to a legal position of the board.

2.2.2 Water Jug Problem:

Water Jug Problem: You are given two jugs: a 4-gallon one & a 3-gallon one, a pump which has unlimited water which you can use to fill the jug, and the ground on which water may be poured. Neither jug has any measuring markings on it. How can you get exactly 2 gallons of water in the 4-gallon jug?

State Space Representation: We will represent a state of the problem as a tuple (x, y) where x represents the amount of water in the 4-gallon jug and y represents the amount of water in the 3-gallon jug. Note that $0 \leq x \leq 4$, and $0 \leq y \leq 3$.

Initial state is (0, 0).

Goal state is (2, n) for any value of n. Note that $0 \leq n \leq 3$.

To solve this problem, we have to make some **assumptions** as follows:

- We can fill a jug from the pump.
- We can pour water out of a jug to the ground.
- We can pour water from one jug to another.
- There is no measuring device available.

Rules: We must define a set of rules that will take us from one state to another. They are as follows:

Rule Number	Current State	Next State	Description
1	(x, y) & x < 4	(4, y)	Fill the 4-gallon jug
2	(x, y) & y < 3	(x, 3)	Fill the 3-gallon jug
3	(x, y) & x > 0	(x-d, y)	Pour some water out of the 4-gallon jug
4	(x, y) & x > 0	(0, y)	Empty the 4-gallon jug on the ground
5	(x, y) & y > 0	(x, y-d)	Pour some water out of the 3-gallon jug
6	(x, y) & y > 0	(x, 0)	Empty the 3-gallon jug on the ground

Rule Number	Current State	Next State	Description
7	(x, y) & x + y >= 4 & y > 0	(4, y - (4 - x))	Pour water from the 3-gallon jug into the 4-gallon jug until the 4-gallon jug is full
8	(x, y) & x + y >= 3 & x > 0	(x - (3 - y), 3)	Pour water from the 4-gallon jug into the 3-gallon jug until the 3-gallon jug is full
9	(x, y) & x + y <= 4 & y > 0	(x + y, 0)	Pour all the water from the 3-gallon jug into the 4-gallon jug
10	(x, y) & x + y <= 3 & x > 0	(0, x + y)	Pour all the water from the 4-gallon jug into the 3-gallon jug
11	(0, 2)	(2, 0)	Pour the 2 gallons from 3-gallon jug into the 4-gallon jug
12	(2, y)	---	GOAL STATE

There are several sequences of rules that will solve the problem. **One of the possible solutions** is:

Sr. No.	Gallons in the 4-Gallon Jug	Gallons in the 3-Gallon Jug	#Rule Applied
1	0	0	2
2	0	3	9
3	3	0	2
4	3	3	7
5	4	2	4
6	0	2	9 or 11
7	2	0	GOAL STATE

2.2.3 8 Puzzle Problem:

The 8 Puzzle Problem: The 8 puzzle consists of eight numbered, movable tiles set in a 3x3 frame. One cell of the frame is always empty thus making it possible to move an adjacent numbered tile into the empty cell. Such a puzzle is illustrated in following figure:

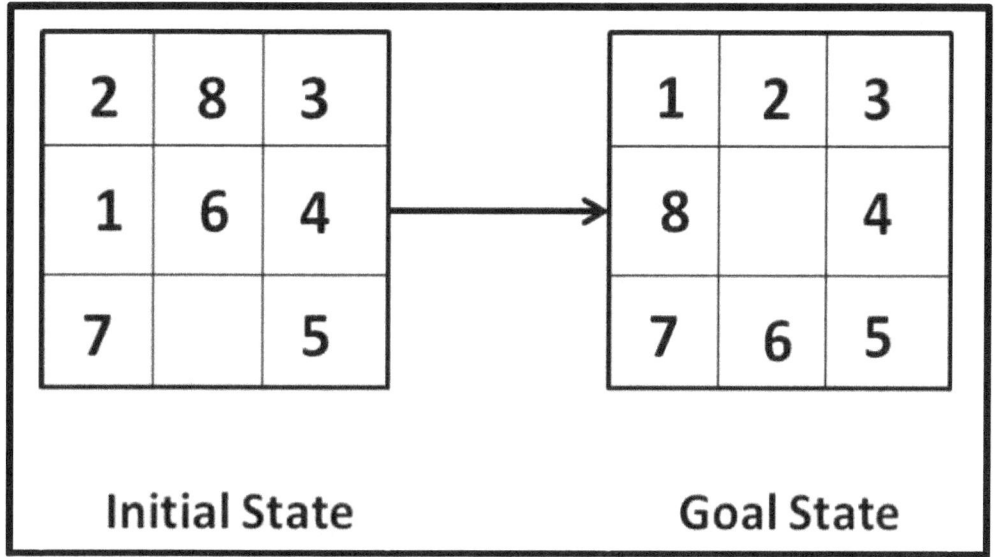

Figure 2.2: 8 Puzzle Problem

The problem is to change the initial state into the goal state. *A solution* to the problem is an appropriate **sequence of moves**, such as "move tiles 5 to the right, move tile 7 to the left, move tile 6 to the down, etc."

Initial states can be **more than one**.

Goal state is **single & unique**.

Although a player moves the tiles around the board to change the configuration of tiles, we will define the **legal moves** in terms of **movement of the space**. The space can be moved **up, down, left & right**.

We define the legal moves in terms of **movement of the space** rather than **movement of the tile** in order to keep the **number of rules** to **minimum**.

The solution to the 8 Puzzle Problem is give in the following figure:

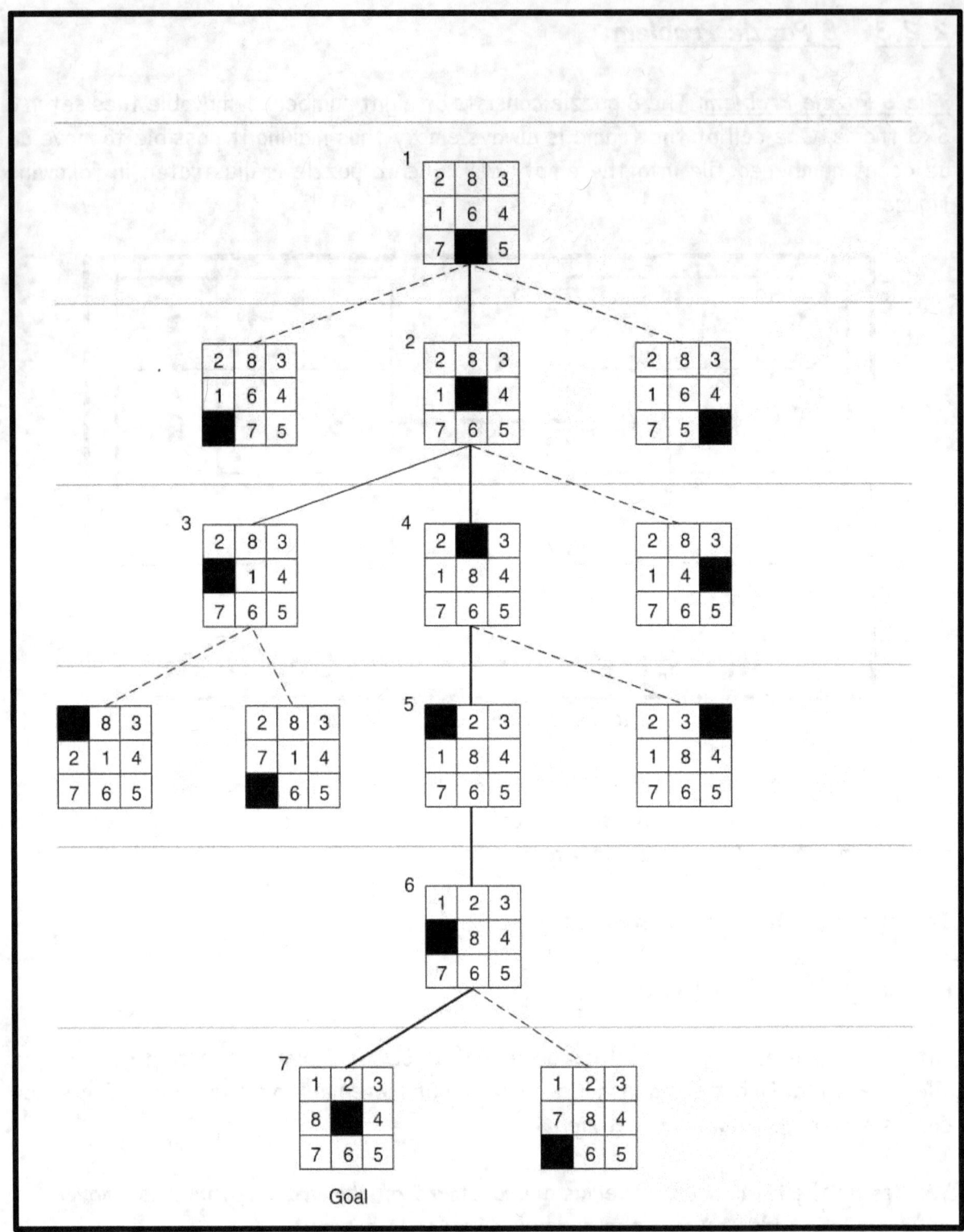

Figure 2.3: 8 Puzzle Problem – Solution Search Tree

2.2.4 Tower of Hanoi Problem:

The Tower of Hanoi Problem: There are three columns and certain rings. The rings are of different sizes & rests over the columns. Initially, all the rings are rested on the leftmost column. The goal is to move all the rings to the rightmost column. The rule is that a larger ring must not be placed on a smaller ring & only one ring can be moved at a time. In the original Tower of Hanoi problem, there are 64 rings but in our case, to clearly understand the problem, we'll use only 2 rings. The solution is as follows:

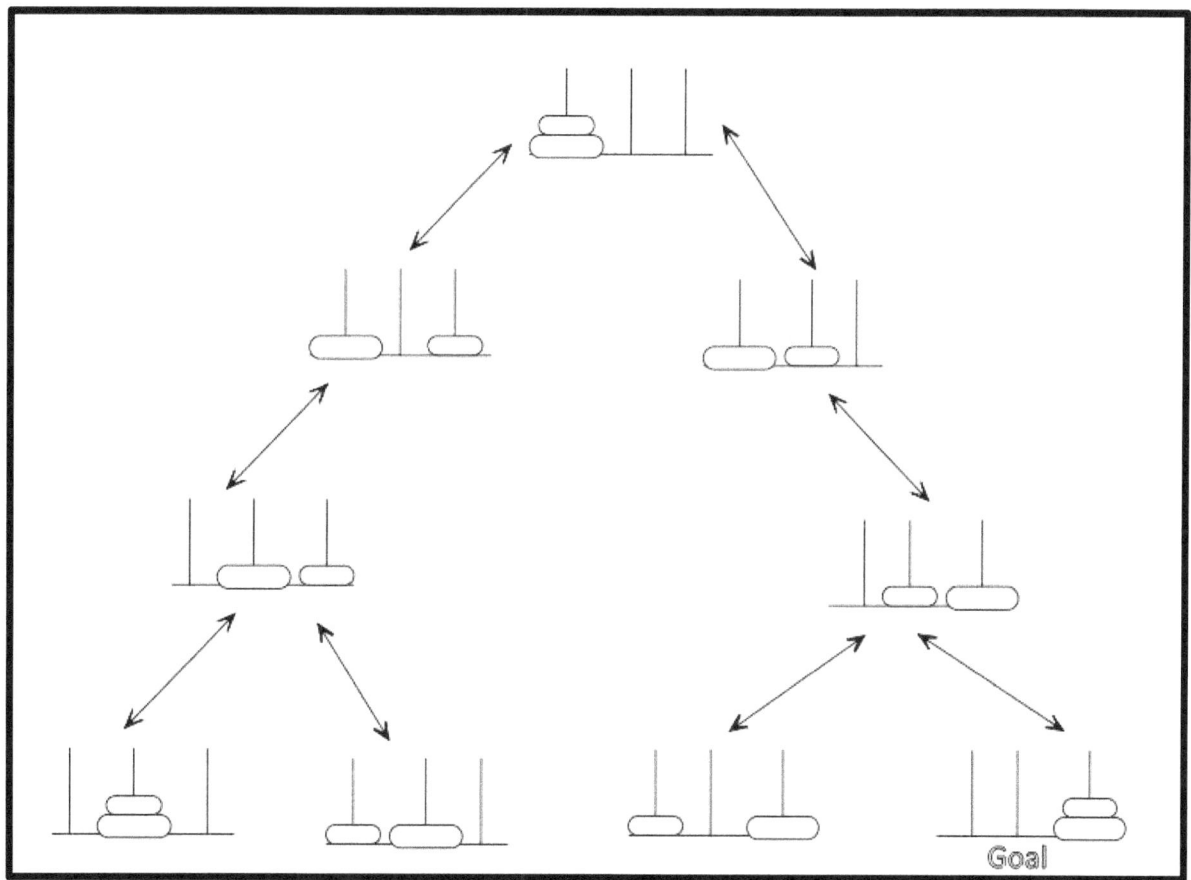

Figure 2.4: Tower of Hanoi Problem – Solution Search Tree

Initial State: Initially, all the rings are on the leftmost column.

Goal State: The goal is to move all the rings to the rightmost column. So, in this problem, we have only one goal state.

Legal Moves: Moves should be defined keeping in mind that a larger ring must not be placed on a smaller ring & only one ring can be moved at a time.

2.2.5 Travelling Salesman Problem:

The Travelling Salesman Problem: Given a list of cities and the distances between each pair of cities, we need to find the shortest possible route that visits each city and returns to the origin city.

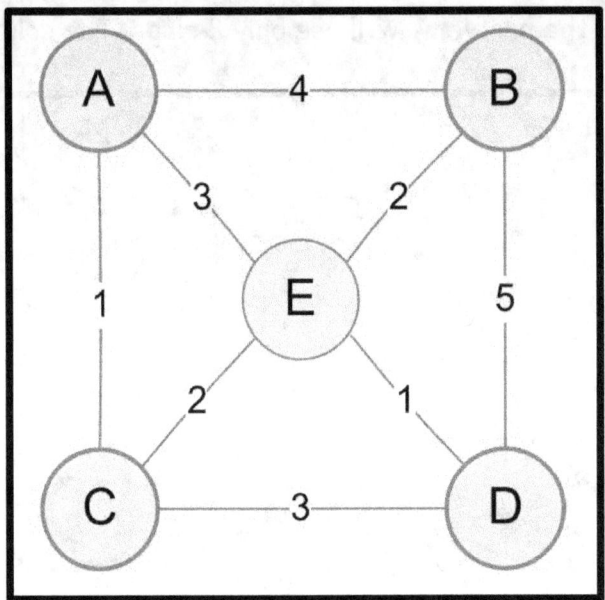

Figure 2.5: Travelling Salesman Problem

Initial State: Any city from the given set of cities.

Goal State: One in which all the cities are visited exactly once & the final city is same as the starting city.

Rules: The trip visits each city exactly once. The trip starts and ends at the same city.

Legal Moves: Next city in the trip should have a direct path from the current city. Select the order of cities in such a way that the overall distance covered in the trip tends to minimum.

The possible solution to the above-mentioned scenario of TSP is given in the following diagram:

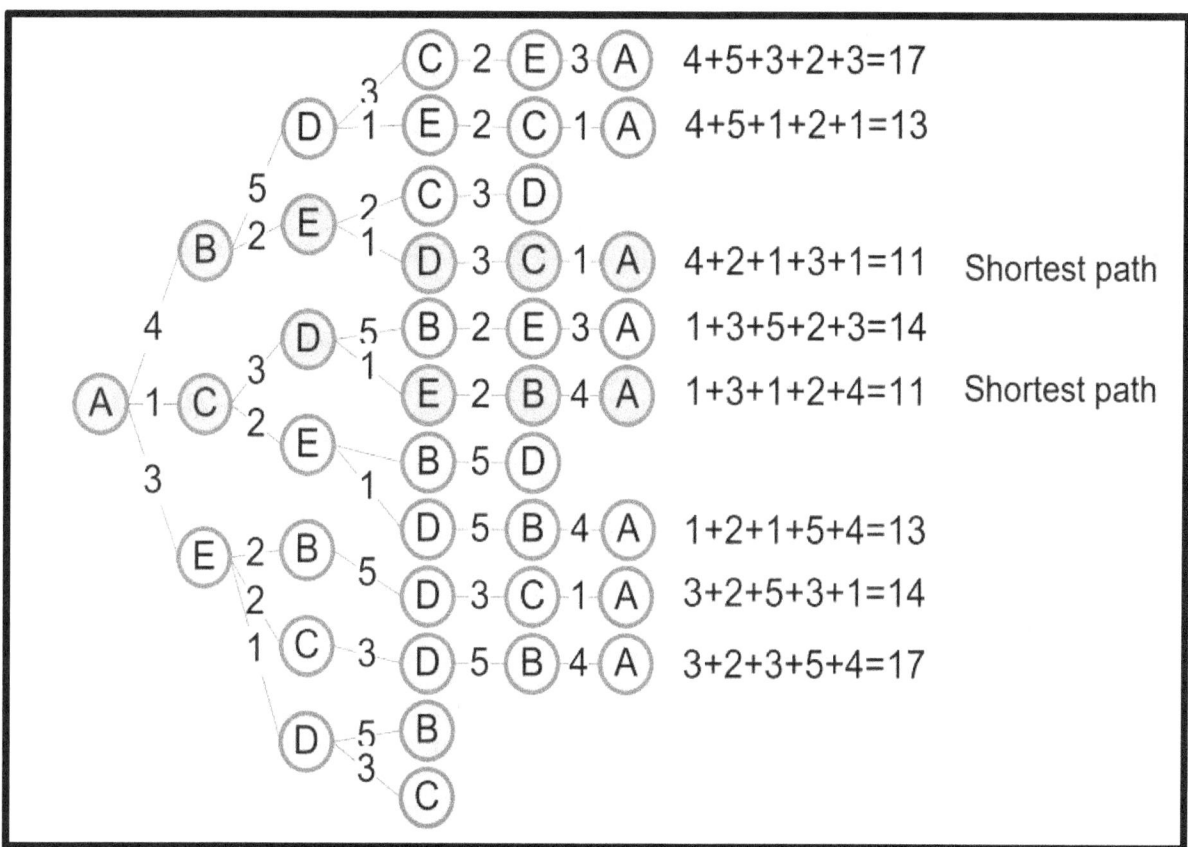

Figure 2.6: Travelling Salesman Problem - Solution Search Tree

2.2.6 8-Queen Problem:

8-Queen Problem: We have 8 queens and an 8 x 8 chessboard having alternate black and white squares. The queens are placed on the chessboard. Any queen can attack any another queen placed on same row, or column, or diagonal. We have to find the proper placement of queens on the chessboard in such a way that no queen attacks other queen.

Initial Sate: The empty 8 x 8 chessboard having alternate black and white squares.

Goal State: Board configuration where none of the queen attacks any of the other queens.

Legal Moves: Placing 8 queens on the chessboard in such a way that goal state is achieved.

Rules: No two queens can be placed on same row, or column, or diagonal.

A possible board configuration to solve the 8-queen problem is as follows:

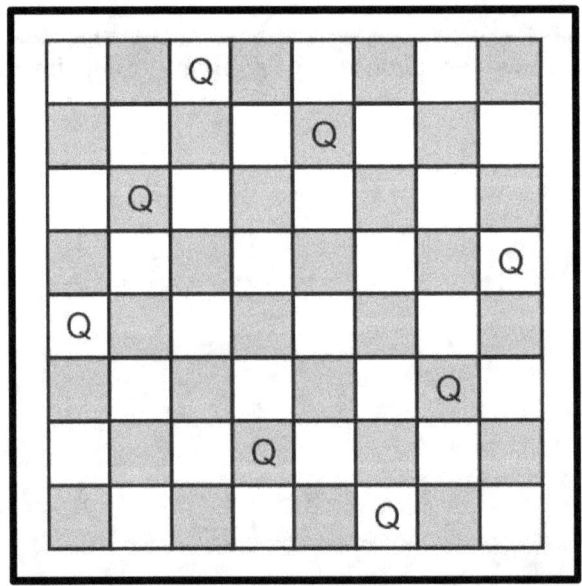

Figure 2.7: 8-Queen Problem - Goal State

2.2.7 Missionaries & Cannibals Problem:

Missionaries & Cannibals Problem: Three missionaries & three cannibals are present at one side of a river and need to cross the river. There is only one boat available. At any point of time, the number of cannibals should not out-number the number of missionaries at that bank. It is also known that only two persons can occupy the boat at a time.

Objective: To find the sequence of transferring missionaries & cannibals from one bank of river to other using the boat sailing through the river satisfying the above stated constraints.

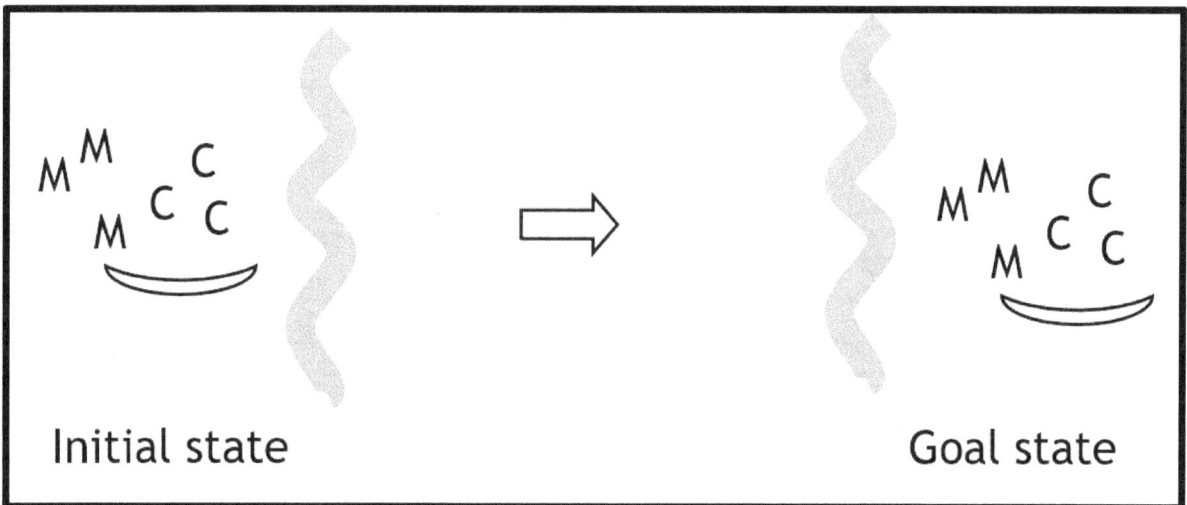

Figure 2.8: Missionaries & Cannibals Problem

Initial State: Three missionaries, three cannibals, & a boat on the left bank of the river. Nothing on the right bank of the river.

Goal State: Three missionaries, three cannibals, & a boat on the right bank of the river. Nothing on the left bank of the river.

Rules: The number of cannibals should not out-number the number of missionaries at that bank. Only two persons can occupy the boat at a time.

We can form various rules as presented in water-jug problem. Let Missionary is denoted by 'M' and Cannibal, by 'C'. These rules are described below:

Rule No.	Boat Status	Description

1	0, M	One missionary sailing the boat from left-bank to right-bank
2	M, 0	One missionary sailing the boat from right-bank to left-bank
3	M, M	Two missionary sailing the boat from left-bank to right-bank
4	M, M	Two missionary sailing the boat from right-bank to left-bank
5	M, C	One missionary & one cannibal sailing the boat from left-bank to right-bank
6	C, M	One missionary & one cannibal sailing the boat from right-bank to left-bank
7	C, C	Two cannibals sailing the boat from left-bank to right-bank
8	C, C	Two cannibals sailing the boat from right-bank to left-bank
9	0, C	One cannibal sailing the boat from left-bank to right-bank
10	C, 0	One cannibal sailing the boat from right-bank to left-bank

The solution to the Missionaries & Cannibals Problem using the above rules is:

Sr. No.	Left-Bank	Right-Bank	Boat Position	#Rule Applied
1	3M, 3C	0M, 0C	Left-Bank	5
2	2M, 2C	1M, 1C	Right-Bank	2
3	3M, 2C	0M, 1C	Left-Bank	7
4	3M, 0C	0M, 3C	Right-Bank	10
5	3M, 1C	0M, 2C	Left-Bank	3
6	1M, 1C	2M, 2C	Right-Bank	6
7	2M, 2C	1M, 1C	Left-Bank	3
8	0M, 2C	3M, 1C	Right-Bank	10
9	0M, 3C	3M, 0C	Left-Bank	7
10	0M, 1C	3M, 2C	Right-Bank	10
11	0M, 2C	3M, 1C	Left-Bank	7
12	0M, 0C	3M, 3C	Right-Bank	-

The possible solution to the Missionaries & Cannibals Problem is given in the following diagram:

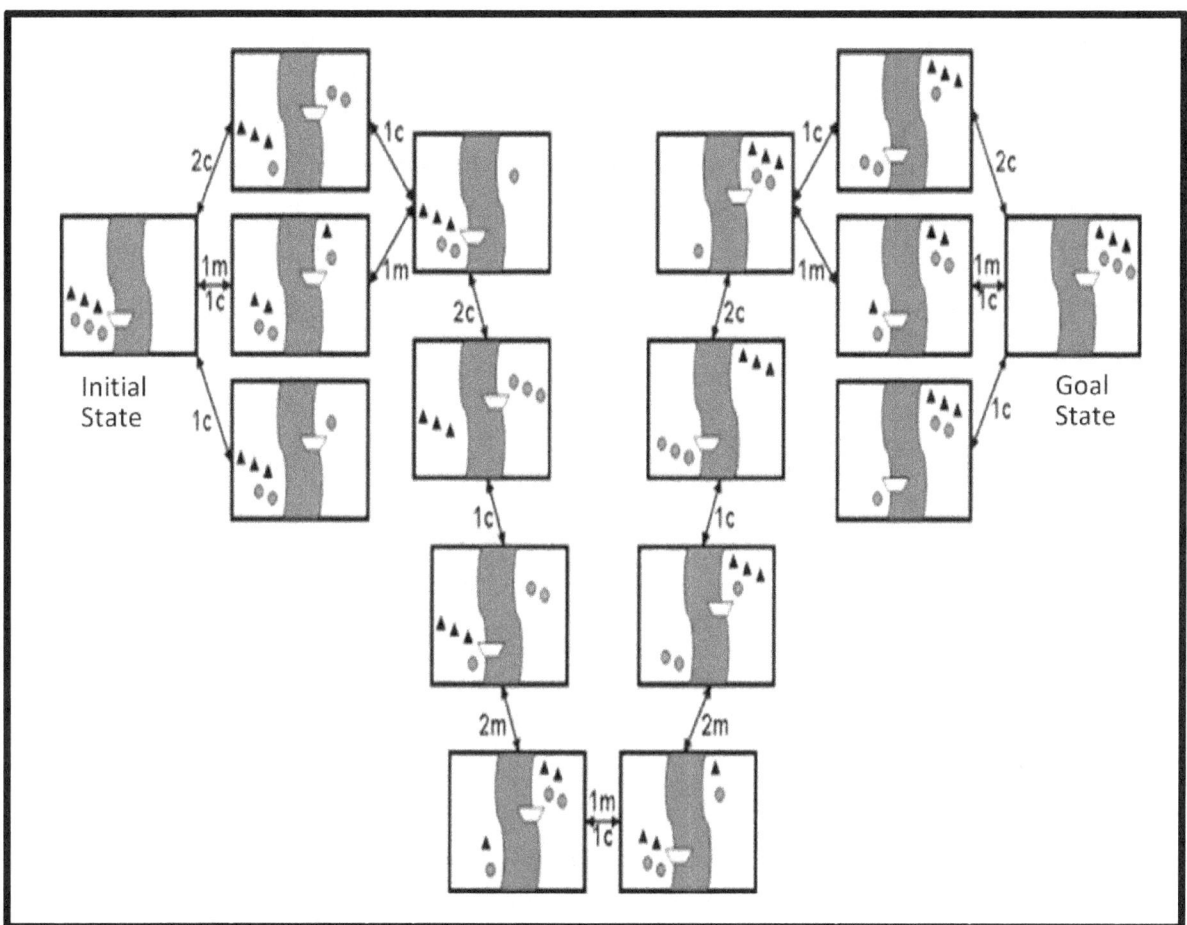

Figure 2.9: Missionaries & Cannibals Problem - Solution Search Tree

2.2.8 Monkey & Banana Problem:

Monkey & Banana Problem: A monkey and a bunch of banana are present in a room. The bananas are hanging from the ceiling. The monkey cannot reach the bananas directly. However, in the room there is one box. The monkey can reach the banana standing on the box. We have to find the sequence of events by which monkey can reach the bananas.

Objects in this scenario are the monkey, the box & the bananas.

To represent the relationship between these objects, we'll represent initial state & goal state as follows:

Initial State:

On (monkey, floor),
On (box, floor),
At (monkey, a),
At (box, b),
At (bananas, c),
Status (bananas, hanging)

Goal State:

On (monkey, box),
On (box, floor),
At (monkey, c),
At (box, c),
At (bananas, c),
Status (bananas, grabbed)

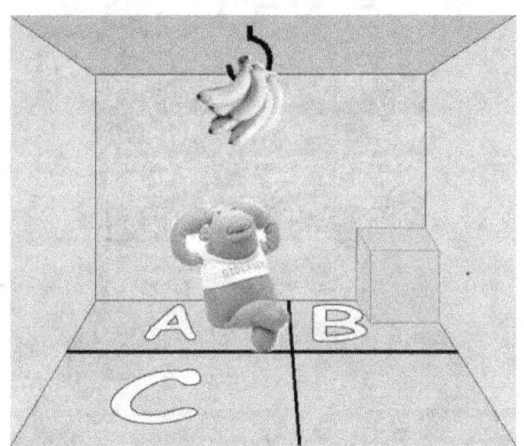

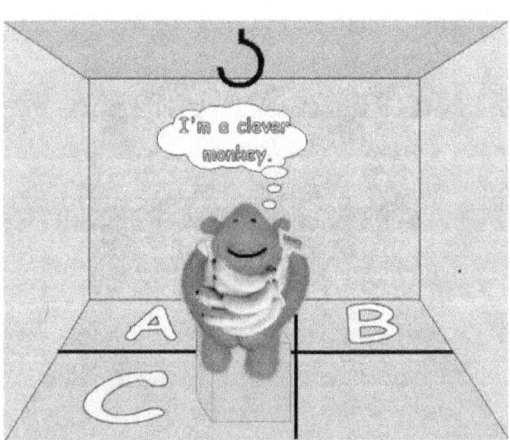

Figure 2.10: The Monkey & Banana Problem

2.2.9 Cryptarithmetic Puzzle:

Cryptarithmetic Puzzle: Each letter in a cryptarithmetic puzzle represents a different digit. No two letters have the same value. The goal is to guess the correct numeric value of the letters, provided the given puzzle. This is a problem of **constraint satisfaction**.

Initial State: Value for none of the letters is known.

Goal State: Values for all of the letters are known.

Constrains: Digits assigned to the letter should be between 0 to 9. No two digit can be assigned to same letter.

Some of the common cryptarithmetic puzzles are:

```
   SEND              DONALD
+ MORE            + GERALD
----------        ----------
  MONEY             ROBERT
```

```
         CROSS
       + ROADS
       ------------
         DANGER
```

```
   BASE               EAT
+  BALL            + THAT
---------         ----------
  GAMES             APPLE
```

Consider the following example of a cryptarithmetic puzzle:

Solve the following Cryptarithmetic problem:

```
  E A T
+ T H A T
---------
A P P L E
```

- Initial guess, A = 1, because the sum of two single digits can generate at most a carry of '1'.

- T = 9 & C3 = 1.

- Thus, P = 0. E + H = 10, C2 = 0.

- A=1. Thus, A+A = L = 2/3.

- We have T=9. Thus, T + T = 18. Thus, E = 8, C1 = 1 & L = 3.

- E + H = 10. Thus, H = 2.

Thus, we have our probable solution as follows:

```
  E A T            819
+ T H A T       + 9219
---------       -------
A P P L E        10038
```

Figure 2.11: Cryptarithmetic Puzzle – Search Tree

2.2.10 Blocks World Problem:

Blocks World Problem: There are some cubic blocks, out of which, each is placed either on the table or on another block forming a particular configuration. We have to move the blocks to arrange them to form some other given configuration by applying minimum number of moves. The requirement of moving a block is that only one block can be moved at a time. Thus, a block that has another block on its top can't be moved. Block can be placed either on the table or on top of any other block.

Consider the following blocks world problem:

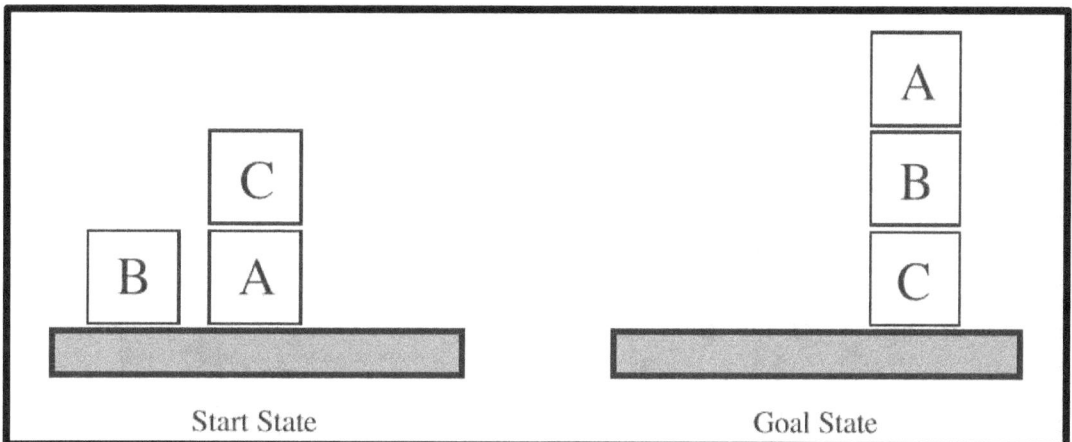

Figure 2.12: Blocks World Problem

2.2.11 Tic-Tac-Toe (Xs & Os) Problem:

Tic-Tac-Toe (Xs and Os) Problem: Tic-tac-toe (also known as Xs and Os) is a game for two players, X and O, who take turns marking the spaces in a 3×3 grid. The player who succeeds in placing three of their marks in a horizontal, vertical, or diagonal row wins the game.

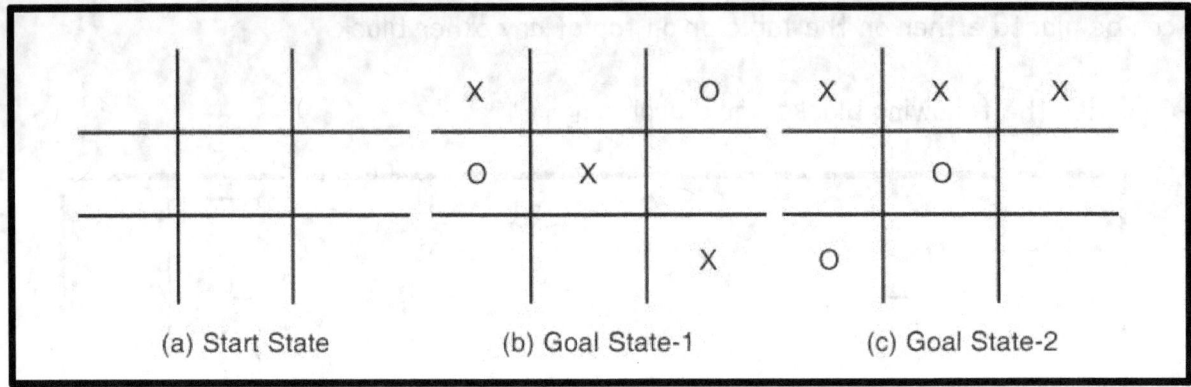

Figure 2.13: Tic-Tac-Toe (Xs & Os) Problem

Initial State: Board position of 3x3 matrix with no Xs & Os.

Goal State: Board position of 3x3 matrix with either three Xs or Os in a horizontal, vertical, or diagonal row.

Legal Moves: Putting O's or X's in vacant positions alternatively.

2.3 AI Problem Characteristics:

In order to choose the most appropriate problem solving method, it is necessary to analyze the problem along various key dimensions. These dimensions are referred to as **problem characteristic**. They are discussed below:

I. Is the problem decomposable?

A very large and composite problem can be easily solved if it can be broken down into smaller sub-problems.

II. Can solution steps be ignored or undone if they prove unwise?

Problem fall under three classes:

- **Ignorable**, in which solution steps can be ignored. Such problems can be solved using a simple control structure that never needs backtracking. Example of Ignorable problem is **Theorem Proving**.

- **Recoverable**, in which solution steps can be undone. Such problems can be solved by a slightly more complex control strategy that allows backtracking. Example of Recoverable problem is **8-Puzzle**.

- **Irrecoverable**, in which solution steps cannot be undone. Such problems need to be solved by a system that expends a great deal of effort making each decision since decision must be final. Example of Irrecoverable problem is **Chess**.

III. Is the problem universe predictable?

Problems can be classified into two types:

- **Certain Outcome**: Examples of problem with certain outcome are **8-puzzle** & **water jug**.

- **Uncertain Outcome**: Examples of problem with uncertain outcome are **playing cards** & **chess**.

IV. Is a good solution to the problem absolute or relative?

- **_Absolute Solution_**: It is the kind of solution in which once you get a solution, you do not need to bother about any other possible solutions.

- **_Relative Solution_**: It is the kind of solution in which once you get a solution, you have to find other possible solutions to check which one is the best.

V. Is the desired solution a state or a path to a state?

- **_Solution as a State_**: Consider the problem of **_natural language processing_** where we need to find the interpretation of some statement. In such problems, we are **only concerned with the interpretation**, **not the steps** that led to that interpretation. Such kind of solutions are a **_State_**.

- **_Solution as a Path to a State_**: Consider the **_water jug problem_**. In such problems, getting the output is not the only objective. Here, **we need to demonstrate the steps** that are carried out to fill the jug-A with 2 gallons of water. Such kind of solutions are **_Path to a State_**.

VI. What is the role of Knowledge?

Is a large amount of knowledge absolutely required to solve the problem, or it is important only to filter the search?

- **_Knowledge Not Absolutely Necessary_**: Consider the problem of playing chess. Just the rules for determining legal moves & some simple control mechanism is sufficient to arrive at a solution. In such problems, large amount of knowledge from the past would definitely help filter the search for better solution but is not absolutely necessary.

- **_Knowledge Absolutely Necessary_**: Consider the problem of predicting the political favoritism by scanning the daily-newspapers. These kinds of problems require enormous amount of knowledge even to predict the solution, let alone the best solution.

VII. Does the task require human interaction?

Can a computer that is simply given the problem return the solution, or will the solution of the problem require interaction between the computer and a person?

> **_Solitary Problems_**: The ones where the computer will be given a problem description and will produce an answer, with no intermediate communication. **_Simple Theorem Proving_** problems fall under this category.

> **_Conversational Problems_**: The ones where there is intermediate communication between a person and the computer, either to provide additional assistance to the computer or to provide additional information to the user, or both. Problems such as **_Medical Diagnosis_** fall under this category.

Some of the common AI problems are described in the following section along with their characteristics:

Playing Chess:

Characteristics	Answer	Description
Is problem decomposable?	No	Problem can't be broken down into sub-problems
Can the solution be ignored or undone?	No	Previous steps can't be undone
Is problem universe predictable?	No	There are multiple possible outcomes
Is the solution absolute or relative?	Absolute	Once you get the solution, other possible solutions don't matter
Is the solution state or path to a state?	Path	The solution is a path to the goal state
What's the role of knowledge?	---	Helps to filter the search but not absolutely necessary
Does the task needs human intervention?	Yes	Additional assistance is required to make a move against the AI

Water Jug:

Characteristics	Answer	Description
Is problem decomposable?	No	Problem can't be broken down into sub-problems
Can the solution be ignored or undone?	Yes	Previous steps can be undone
Is problem universe predictable?	Yes	There is only a single possible outcome
Is the solution absolute or relative?	Absolute	Once you get the solution, other possible solutions don't matter
Is the solution state or path to a state?	Path	The solution is a path to the goal state
What's the role of knowledge?	---	Helps to filter the search but not absolutely necessary
Does the task needs human intervention?	Yes	Additional assistance is required to operate the pump

8-Puzzle:

Characteristics	Answer	Description
Is problem decomposable?	No	Problem can't be broken down into sub-problems
Can the solution be ignored or undone?	Yes	Previous steps can be undone
Is problem universe predictable?	Yes	There is only a single possible outcome
Is the solution absolute or relative?	Absolute	Once you get the solution, other possible solutions don't matter
Is the solution state or path to a state?	Path	The solution is a path to the goal state
What's the role of knowledge?	---	Helps to filter the search but not absolutely necessary
Does the task needs human intervention?	No	No additional assistance is required

Travelling Salesman:

Characteristics	Answer	Description
Is problem decomposable?	No	Problem can't be broken down into sub-problems
Can the solution be ignored or undone?	No	Previous steps can't be undone
Is problem universe predictable?	No	There are multiple possible outcomes
Is the solution absolute or relative?	Relative	We have to find all the paths to find the shortest path
Is the solution state or path to a state?	Path	The solution is a path to the goal state
What's the role of knowledge?	---	Helps to filter the search but not absolutely necessary
Does the task needs human intervention?	No	No additional assistance is required

Missionaries & Cannibals:

Characteristics	Answer	Description
Is problem decomposable?	No	Problem can't be broken down into sub-problems
Can the solution be ignored or undone?	Yes	Previous steps can be undone
Is problem universe predictable?	Yes	There is only a single possible outcome
Is the solution absolute or relative?	Absolute	Once you get the solution, other possible solutions don't matter
Is the solution state or path to a state?	Path	The solution is a path to the goal state
What's the role of knowledge?	---	Helps to filter the search but not absolutely necessary
Does the task needs human intervention?	Yes	Additional assistance is required to operate the boat

Tower of Hanoi:

Characteristics	Answer	Description
Is problem decomposable?	No	Problem can't be broken down into sub-problems
Can the solution be ignored or undone?	Yes	Previous steps can be undone
Is problem universe predictable?	Yes	There is only a single possible outcome
Is the solution absolute or relative?	Absolute	Once you get the solution, other possible solutions don't matter
Is the solution state or path to a state?	Path	The solution is a path to the goal state
What's the role of knowledge?	---	Helps to filter the search but not absolutely necessary
Does the task needs human intervention?	No	No additional assistance is required

2.4 Production System:

Search process forms the core of many AI processes. So, it is important to structure AI programs in a way that facilitates the search process. **Production System** provides such structures.

A production system consists of:

- **A set of rules**, each consisting of a left side (a pattern) that determines the applicability of the rule and a right side that describes the operation to be performed if the rule is applied.

- **One or more knowledge/databases** that contain whatever information is appropriate for the particular task.

- **A control strategy** that specifies the order in which the rules will be compared to the database and a way of resolving the conflicts that arise when several rules match at once.

- **A rule applier** that implements the control strategy and applies the rules.

In order to solve a problem, we must first reduce it to the form for which a precise statement can be given. This can be done by defining the problem's **state space**. The problem can then be solved by searching for a path through the space from an **initial state** to a **goal state**. This process of solving the problem can usefully be modeled as a **production system**.

2.5 Issues in the Design of Search Programs:

Every **search process** can be viewed as a **traversal of a tree** structure in which each node represents a problem state and each arc represents a relationship between the states it connects.

To carry out the search process, we must first discuss the **issues in design of search programs**:

- **The direction** in which to conduct the search (**forward versus backward reasoning**). We can search forward through the state space from the start state to a goal state, or we can search backward from the goal.

- **Flow to select applicable rules** (**matching**). It is critical to have efficient procedures for matching rules against states.

- **How to represent each node** of the search process (**knowledge representation**).

2.6 Control Strategies:

Control strategies help us decide ***which rule to apply next*** during the ***process of searching*** for a solution to a problem. A ***good control strategy*** should have the ***following characteristics***:

- ***It should cause motion***: Consider the water jug problem discussed previously. Suppose that the control strategy starts each time at the top of the list of rules and chooses the first applicable rule. If we did that, we would never solve the problem. Thus, the control strategies that does not causes motion will never solve the problem.

- ***It should be Systematic***: Consider the water jug problem discussed previously. Suppose that the control strategy starts each time at the top of the list of rules and chooses a rule randomly from applicable rules. This strategy causes motion & it will come to a solution eventually but we're likely to arrive at the same state during the process. This will consume relatively more time to arrive at a solution. Thus, the control strategies that are not systematic will increase the time complexity of the search.

Control strategies are classified in to the following ***two types***:

1. ***Brute-Force / Undirected Search Control Strategy***: The ***uninformed*** or ***undirected*** or ***blind*** or ***brute-force*** search is the search methodology having no additional information about states beyond that provided in the problem definition. In this search, total search space is looked for solution. Examples of this kind of search are ***Breadth-First Search (BFS), Depth-First Search (DFS), Depth-Limited search (DLS) & Bidirectional Search***.

2. ***Heuristic / Directed Search Control Strategy***: These are the search techniques where additional information about the problem is provided in order to guide the search in a specific direction. Examples of this kind of search are ***Best-First Search, Hill Climbing, Constraint Satisfaction, Problem Reduction***, ***etc.***

Both of these types & their techniques are discussed in the following section of the chapter.

2.7 Brute-Force / Undirected Search Control Strategy:

The **uninformed** or **undirected** or **blind** or **brute-force** search is the search methodology having **no additional information about states** beyond that provided in the problem definition. In this search, **total search space is looked for solution**.

Examples of this kind of search are **Breadth-First Search (BFS), Depth-First Search (DFS), Depth-Limited search (DLS) & Bidirectional Search**.

2.7.1 Breadth-First Search:

In this type of search, the state space is represented in form of a tree. The solution is obtained by traversing through the tree & expanding it. The nodes of tree represent **start state**, various **intermediate states & the goal state**.

While searching for the solution, the **tree is traversed & expanded breadth-wise (level-wise)**, that is, only after a level has fully been expanded we go on with the next level. This is where the method's name comes from.

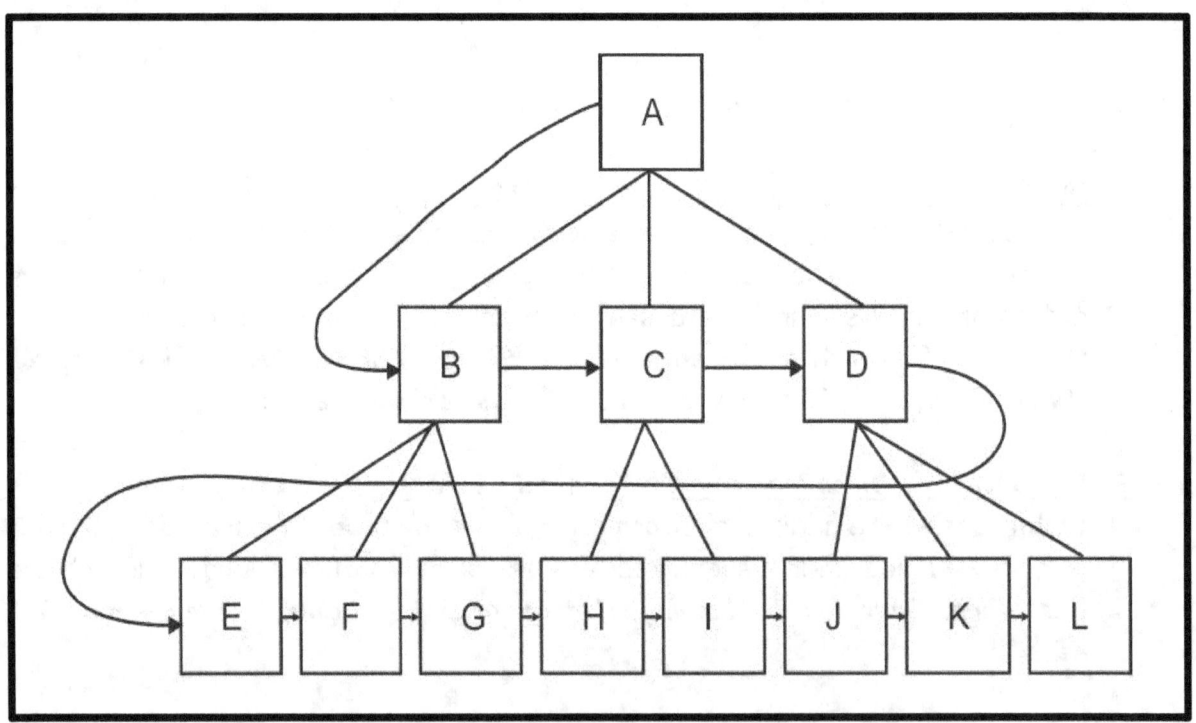

Figure 2.14: Breadth-First Search Tree

For the above figure, the **traversal / expansion order** will be: **A, B, C, D, E, F, G, H, I, J, K, L**.

In *breadth-first search (BFS)*, the *space complexity is more critical* as compared to time complexity. The problems involving search of exponential space complexity (like *chess game*) can't be solved by uninformed methods for the simple reason, the size of the data being too big.

The *data structure* used for breadth-first search (BFS) is *First-In First-Out (FIFO)*.

Algorithm for breadth-first search (BFS) is described as follows:

1. Create a variable called Node-List and set it to initial state.
2. Until a goal state is found or Node-List is empty do:

    2.1. Remove the first element from node-list and call it E. If node-list was empty, quit.
    2.2. For each rule that matches the state described in E do:

        2.2.1. Apply the rule to generate a new state.
        2.2.2. If new state is a goal state, quit and return this state.
        2.2.3. Else, add new state to the end of node-list.

Advantages of Breadth-First Search (BFS):

The breadth first search will not follow a single unfruitful path for very long time or forever. In the situations where solution exists, the breadth first search is guaranteed to find it.

Besides this, in the situations where there are multiple solutions, the BFS finds the minimal solution (the one that requires the minimum number of steps). This is because of the fact that in breadth first search, the longer paths are never explored until all shorter ones have already been examined.

Traveling sales person (TSP) problem discussed above can be solved using Breadth-First Search technique. It will simply explore all the paths possible in the tree and will ultimately come out with the shortest path desired. However, this strategy works well only if the number of cities is less. If we have large number of cities in the list, it fails miserably because number of paths and hence the time taken to perform the search become too big to be controlled by this method efficiently.

2.7.2 Depth-First Search:

In this type of approach, instead of traversing / expanding the breadth-wise, we **explore one branch of a tree** until the solution is found or we decide to terminate the search because either a dead end is met or the process becomes longer than the set time limit. If any of the above situations is encountered & the **process is terminated**, **a backtracking occurs. A fresh search will be done on some other branch** of the tree, and the process will be **repeated until goal state is reached**. This type of technique is known as **depth-first search (DFS)** technique.

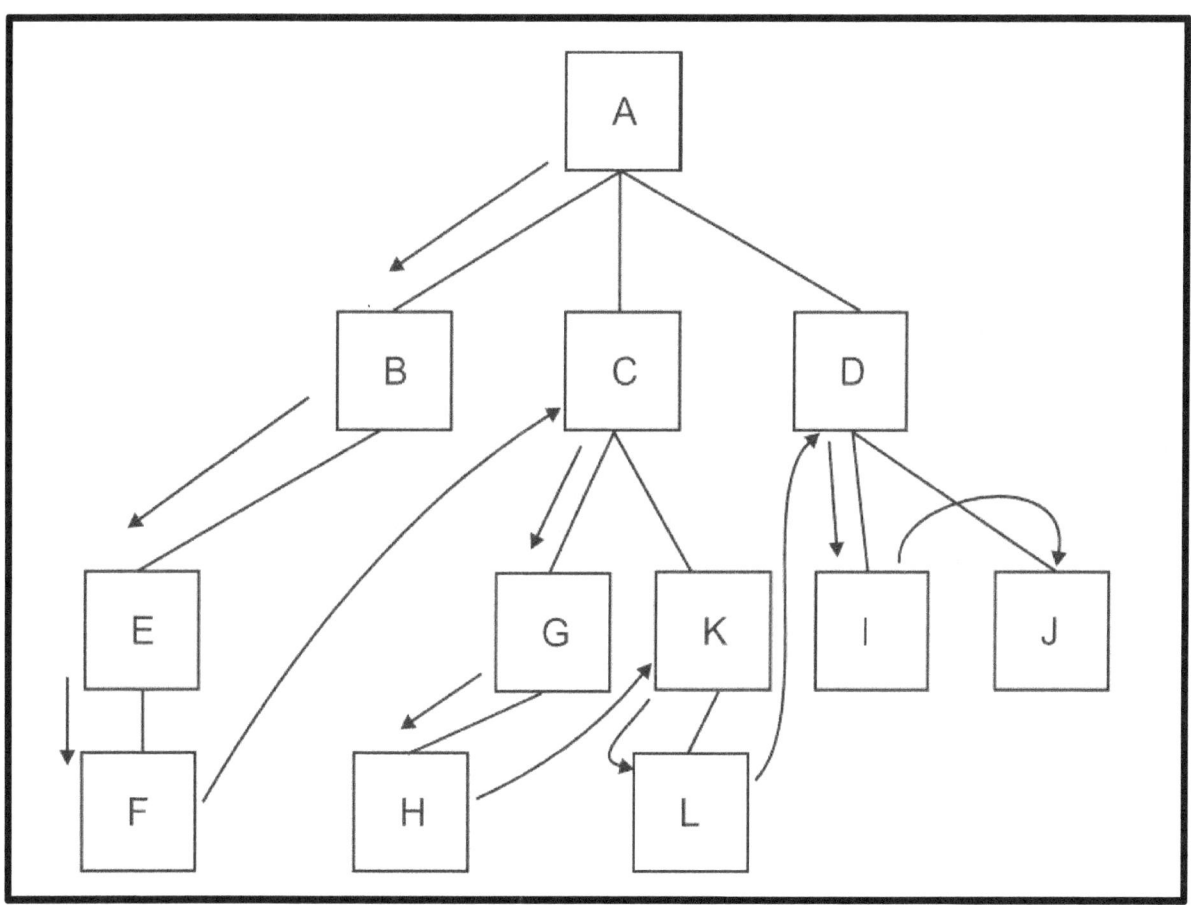

Figure 2.15: Depth-First Search Tree

For the above figure, the **traversal / expansion order** will be: **A, B, E, F, C, G, H, K, L, D, I & J.**

The **depth-first search (DFS)** has <u>lesser space complexity</u>, because at a time it needs to store only single path from root to leaf node.

The <u>data structure</u> used for **depth-first search (DFS)** is **Last-In First-Out (LIFO)**.

Depth-first search (DFS) technique is implemented recursively using a *recursion stack*.

Algorithm for depth-first search (DFS) is described as follows:

> 1. Create a variable called Node-List and set it to initial state.
> 2. Until a goal state is found or Node-List is empty do:
>
>   2.1. Remove the first element from node-list and call it E. If node-list was empty, quit.
>   2.2. For each rule that matches the state described in E do:
>
>   2.2.1. Apply the rule to generate a new state.
>   2.2.2. If new state is a goal state, quit and return this state.
>   2.2.3. Else, add new state to the start of node-list.

Unlike **breadth-first search (BFS)**, we may **quickly find goal state using depth-first search (DFS)**, even if the goal state is deep in the tree. But there's **no guarantee that the found solution is optimal**. This is because **depth-first search (DFS) returns the first solution** that it encounters without comparing it to any other possible solutions.

2.7.3 Breadth-First Search versus Depth-First Search:

Sr. No.	Breadth-First Search	Depth-First Search
1	BFS starts traversal from the root node & then explore the search in the level by level manner.	DFS starts traversal from the root node & explores one branch of a tree until the solution is found or search is terminated.
2	BFS requires significant memory resources because it needs to store all the paths from root node to leaf node.	DFS requires lesser memory resources because at a time it needs to store only single path from root to leaf node.
3	BFS takes more time to reach the goal state.	DFS takes less time to reach the goal state.
4	If there is a solution, BFS is guaranteed to find it.	DFS in not guaranteed to find the solution.
5	Optimal solution is guaranteed.	Optimal solution is not guaranteed.
6	BFS uses FIFO (First-In First-Out) data structure.	DFS uses LIFO (Last-In First-Out) data structure.
7	BFS uses queue data structure.	DFS uses stack data structure.
8	BFS does not require Recursion.	DFS requires Recursion.
9	BFS does not require Backtracking.	DFS requires Backtracking.
10	```
      A
     / \
    B   C
   /   / \
  D   E   F
```  A, B, C, D, E, F | ```
      A
     / \
    B   C
   /   / \
  D   E   F
```  A, B, D, C, E, F |

2.8 Heuristic / Directed Search Control Strategy:

Heuristic / Directed / Informed search control strategies are the search techniques where *additional information about the problem is provided* in order to guide the search in a specific direction. These techniques know whether one non-goal state is more promising than another or not.

Examples of this kind of search are *Generate-And-Test*, *Best-First Search*, *Hill Climbing*, *Constraint Satisfaction*, *Problem Reduction*, *Means-End-Analysis*, etc.

2.8.1 Generate-And-Test:

The generate-and-test strategy is the simplest of all the Heuristic approaches we will discuss. *Algorithm* for the *generate-and-test* strategy is as follows:

1. *Generate a possible solution. For some problems, this means generating a particular configuration in the problem space. For others, it means generating a path to that configuration from initial configuration.*

2. *Test to see if this is actually a solution by comparing it to the set of acceptable goal states.*

3. *If a solution has been found, quit. Else, return to step 1.*

If the generation of possible solutions is done systematically, then **this procedure will find a solution eventually**, if it exists. Unfortunately, if the problem space is very large, this method **takes a very long time** to find the solution.

The most straightforward way to *implement a systematic generate-and-test* is as a *depth-first search tree with backtracking* because complete solutions must be generated before they can be tested.

In its most systematic form, *generate-and-test* is simply an *exhaustive search of the problem space* & operates by generating solutions randomly.

2.8.2 Hill Climbing:

Hill climbing is a variant of generate-and-test in which **feedback from the test procedure** is used to help the generator **decide which direction to move in the search space**.

If the **test function is merged with a heuristic function** that provides an **estimate of how close a given state is to a goal state**, the generate procedure can exploit it to **direct the search in the right direction**. This is what **Hill Climbing** does.

Hill climbing is often used when a good **heuristic function** is available for evaluating states but when **no other useful knowledge is available. For example**, suppose you are in an unfamiliar city without a map and you want to get downtown. You simply aim for the tall buildings. The heuristic function is just distance between the current location & the location of the tall buildings.

2.8.2.1 Simple Hill Climbing:

Algorithm for *Simple Hill Climbing*:

1. Evaluate the initial state. If it is also goal state, then return it and quit. Else, continue with the initial state as the current state.
2. Loop until a solution is found or until a complete iteration produces no change to current state:

   2.1. Select a rule that hasn't yet been applied to the current state and apply it to produce a new state.
   2.2. Evaluate the new state

      2.2.1. If it is the goal state, then return it and quit.
      2.2.2. If it is not a goal state but it is better than the current state, then make it the current state.
      2.2.3. If it is not better than the current state, then continue in the loop.

2.8.2.2 Steepest-Ascent Hill Climbing:

Steepest-Ascent Hill Climbing is a variation of simple hill climbing that **considers all the possible moves from the current state & selects the best one** as the next state. Notice that this method **contrasts with the simple hill climbing** method in which the first state that is better than the current state is selected.

Algorithm for **Steepest-Ascent Hill Climbing**:

1. Evaluate the initial state. If it is also goal state, then return it and quit. Else, continue with the initial state as the current state.
2. Loop until a solution is found or until a complete iteration produces no change to current state:

    2.1. Let SUCC be a state such that any possible successor of the current state will be better than SUCC.
    2.2. For each rule that applies to the current state do:

        2.2.1. Apply the operator and generate a new state.
        2.2.2. Evaluate the new state. If it is a goal state, then return it and quit. If not, compare it to SUCC. If it is better, then set SUCC to this state. Else, leave SUCC alone.

    2.3. If the SUCC is better than current state, then set current state to SUCC.

2.8.2.3 Issues in Hill Climbing:

Both **simple & steepest-ascent hill climbing may fail to find a solution**. Either algorithm may terminate not by finding a goal state but by getting to a state from which no better states can be generated. This will happen **if the program has reached either a local maximum, a plateau, or a ridge**.

- A *local maximum* is a state that is better than all its neighbors but is not better than some other states farther away. At a local maximum, all moves appear to make things worse.

- A *plateau* is a flat area of the search space in which a whole set of neighboring states have the same value. On a plateau, it is not possible to determine the best direction in which to move by making local comparisons.

- A *ridge* is an area which is higher than surrounding states, but it can't be reached in a single move; for example, we have four possible directions to explore (N, E, W, S) and an area exists in NE direction

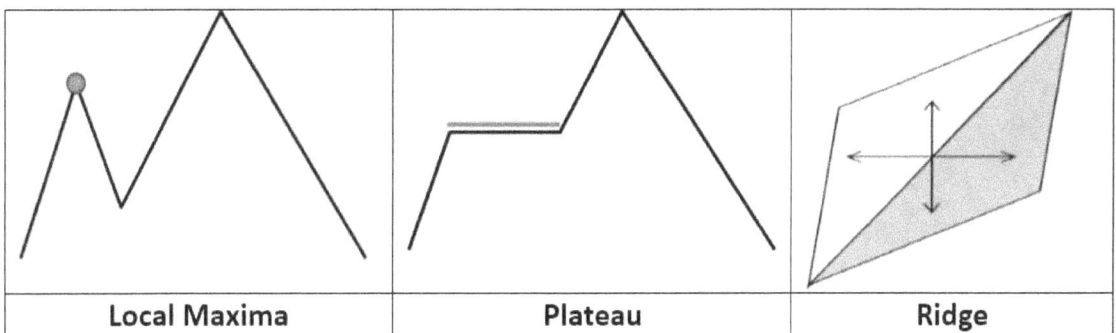

Figure 2.16: Issues in Hill Climbing

The **solutions to these problems** are stated below:

- *Local Maximum Problem*: **Backtrack to some earlier node and try going in a different direction.** This is particularly reasonable if at that node there was another direction that looked as promising or almost as promising as the one that was chosen earlier. To implement this strategy, maintain a list of paths almost taken and go back to one of them if the path that was taken leads to a dead end. This is a fairly good way of dealing with **local maxima**.

- **_Plateau Problem_**: ***Make a big jump in some direction to try to get to a new section of the search space***. If the only rules available describe single small steps, apply them several times in the same direction. This is a particularly good way of dealing with **plateaus**.

- **_Ridge Problem_**: ***Apply two or more rules before doing the test***. This corresponds to **moving in several directions at once**. This is a particularly good strategy for dealing with **ridges**.

2.8.2.4 *Simulated Annealing*:

Simulated annealing is a variation of hill climbing in which, at the beginning of the process, *some downhill moves may be made*. This should lower the chances of getting caught at a *local maximum, a plateau, or a ridge*.

Simulated annealing is patterned after the *physical process of annealing*, in which *physical substances such as metals are melted* (i.e., raised to high energy levels) & then *gradually cooled until some solid state is reached*.

We make *two notational changes* for the duration of this topic.

- We use the term *objective function* in place of the term *heuristic function*.

- And we attempt to *minimize rather than maximize the value of the objective function*. Thus, we actually describe a process of *valley descending* rather than *hill climbing*.

The algorithm for *simulated annealing is only slightly different from the simple hill-climbing procedure*. The *three differences* are:

- The *annealing schedule* must be maintained. It refers to the *rate at which the system is cooled*.

- *Moves to worse states* may be accepted.

- It is a good idea to *maintain the best state found so far*. Then, if the next state is worse than that earlier state, the earlier state is still available.

Basically, if the next state is better than the current state, the value of current state is set to next state & the process moves forward.

But if the next state is worse than the current state the process descends from the current state to the previous state in order to take a different path to reach a solution. The idea behind annealing is that, at high temperatures the algorithm should jump out of a local maxima.

Algorithm for **_Simulated Annealing_**:

1. Evaluate the initial state. If it is also goal state, then return it and quit. Else, continue with the initial state as the current state.
2. Initialize BEST-SO-FAR to the current state.
3. Initialize T as per the annealing schedule.
4. Loop until a solution is found or until a complete iteration produces no change to current state:

    4.1. Select an operator that has not yet been applied to the current state and apply it to produce a new state.
    4.2. Evaluate the new state.
    Compare, ΔE = (value of current state) - (value of new state):

      4.2.1. If the new state is a goal state, then return it and quit.
      4.2.2. If it is not a goal state but is better than the current state, then make it the current state. Also set BEST-SO-FAR to this new state.
      4.2.3. If it is not better than the current state, then make it the current state with probability p' as defined above. This step is usually implemented by invoking a random number generator to produce a number in the range [0, 1]. If that number is less than p', then the move is accepted. Otherwise, do nothing.

    4.3. Revise T as necessary according to the annealing schedule.

5. Return BEST-SO-FAR, as the answer.

2.8.2.5 *Hill Climbing versus Simulated Annealing:*

Sr. No.	Hill Climbing	Simulated Annealing
1	Hill climbing gradually improves a solution recursively by selecting the best neighbor based on an evaluation function until there is no neighbor left which is better than the current state.	Simulated Annealing emulates the concept in metallurgy; where metals are heated to very high temperature and then gradually cooled so its structure is frozen at a minimum energy configuration.
2	Hill climbing is usually gets stuck in a local maxima, ridges or plateaus.	Simulated annealing is technique that allows downward steps in order to escape from local maxima.
3	Hill Climbing algorithm only accepts a state that is better than the current state.	Simulated Annealing algorithm has the capability to accept the state that is worse than the current state.

2.8.3 Best-First Search:

Depth-First Search (DFS) is good because it allows a solution to be found without expanding all competing branches. **Breadth-First Search (BFS)** is good because it does not get trapped on dead end paths. **Best-First Search** combines the advantages of **both DFS & BFS** into a single method. It *follows a single path at a time, but switches paths whenever some other path looks more promising* than the current one.

Best-first search is an instance of the general **TREE-SEARCH** *algorithm* in which a node is selected for expansion based on a **heuristic function**. The heuristic function is construed as a **cost estimate**, so the **node with the lowest evaluation is expanded first**.

2.8.3.1 OR Graphs:

Usually what happens in **Best-First Search** is that a bit of depth-first searching occurs as the most promising branch is explored. But eventually, if a solution is not found, that branch will start to look less promising than one of the top-level branches that had been ignored.

At that point, the now more promising, **previously ignored branch** will be explored. But the **old branch is not forgotten**. Its last node remains in the set of **generated but unexpanded** nodes. The **search can return to it** whenever all the other branches gets relatively bad. We will call a **graph of this type** as an **OR graph**, since each of its branches represents an alternative problem-solving path.

To implement such a graph-search procedure, we will need to use two **lists of nodes**:

- **OPEN**: Nodes that have been generated and have had the heuristic function applied to them but which have not yet been examined.

- **CLOSED**: Nodes that have already been examined. We need to keep these nodes in memory because whenever a new node is generated; we need to check whether it has been generated before.

2.8.3.2 Best-First Search Algorithm:

1. Start with OPEN containing just the initial state.
2. Until a goal is found or there are no nodes left on OPEN do:

    2.1. Pick the best node on OPEN.
    2.2. Generate its successors.
    2.3. For each successor do:

    2.3.1. If it hasn't been generated before, evaluate it, add it to OPEN, and record its parent.
    2.3.2. If it has been generated before, change the parent if this new path is better than the previous one. In that case, update the cost of getting to this node and to any successors that this node may already have.

2.8.3.3 A* Algorithm:

The **best-first search** algorithm is a **simplification of** an algorithm called **A* Algorithm**. The A* algorithm also uses the OPEN & CLOSED list of nodes that we discussed in the previous section. Along with that, the **A* algorithm** uses the following **functions**:

1. <u>f'</u>: The function f' is an estimate of the **cost of getting from the initial state to a goal state** along with the path that's generated from the current node. f' = g + h'.

2. <u>g</u>: The function g is a measure of the **cost of getting from initial state to the current node**.

3. <u>h'</u>: The function h' is an estimate of the **cost of getting from the current node to a goal state**.

<u>A* Algorithm</u>:

1. Start with OPEN containing only initial node. Set that node's g value to 0, its h' value to whatever it is, and its f' value to h'+0 or h'. Set CLOSED to empty list.
2. Until a goal node is found, repeat the following procedure:
   If there are no nodes on OPEN, report failure. Otherwise select the node on OPEN with the lowest f' value. Call it BESTNODE. Remove it from OPEN. Place it in CLOSED. See if the BESTNODE is a goal state. If so exit and report a solution. Otherwise, generate the successors of BESTNODE but do not set the BESTNODE to point to them yet. For each of the SUCCESSOR, do the following:

   2.1. Set SUCCESSOR to point back to BESTNODE. These backwards links will make it possible to recover the path once a solution is found.
   2.2. Compute g(SUCCESSOR) = g(BESTNODE) + the cost of getting from BESTNODE to SUCCESSOR
   2.3. See if SUCCESSOR is the same as any node on OPEN. If so call the node OLD.

> 2.3.1. Check whether it is cheaper to get to OLD via its current parent or to SUCESSOR via BESTNODE by comparing their g values.
> 2.3.2. If OLD is cheaper, then do nothing. If SUCCESSOR is cheaper then reset OLD's parent link to point to BESTNODE.
> 2.3.3. Record the new cheaper path in g(OLD) and update f'(OLD).
>
> 2.4. If SUCCESSOR was not on OPEN, see if it is on CLOSED. If so, call the node on CLOSED OLD and add OLD to the list of BESTNODE's successors.
> 2.5. If SUCCESSOR was not already on either OPEN or CLOSED, then put it on OPEN and add it to the list of BESTNODE's successors. Compute f'(SUCCESSOR) = g(SUCCESSOR) + h'(SUCCESSOR)

Admissibility of A*:

- A heuristic function h'(n) is said to be *admissible* if it *never overestimates the cost of getting to a goal state*.

- That is, if the true minimum cost of getting from node n to a goal state is C then heuristic function must satisfy: $h'(n) \leq C$

- If h' *never overestimates* the cost, then A* algorithm is guaranteed to find an optimal solution, if one exists.

Applicability of A* Algorithm:

Since the **A* algorithm** guarantees to find the **optimal solution** to a given problem, it can be used to solve the **Travelling Sales Person (TSP)** problem.

It is also used to solve the **8-Puzzle problem**.

For an instance, consider the following **examples of 8-Puzzle problem**:

Example 1: Consider the following initial and goal configuration for 8-puzzle problem. Draw the search tree for initial three iterations of A* (Best First search) algorithm to reach from initial state to goal state. Assume suitable heuristic function for the same.

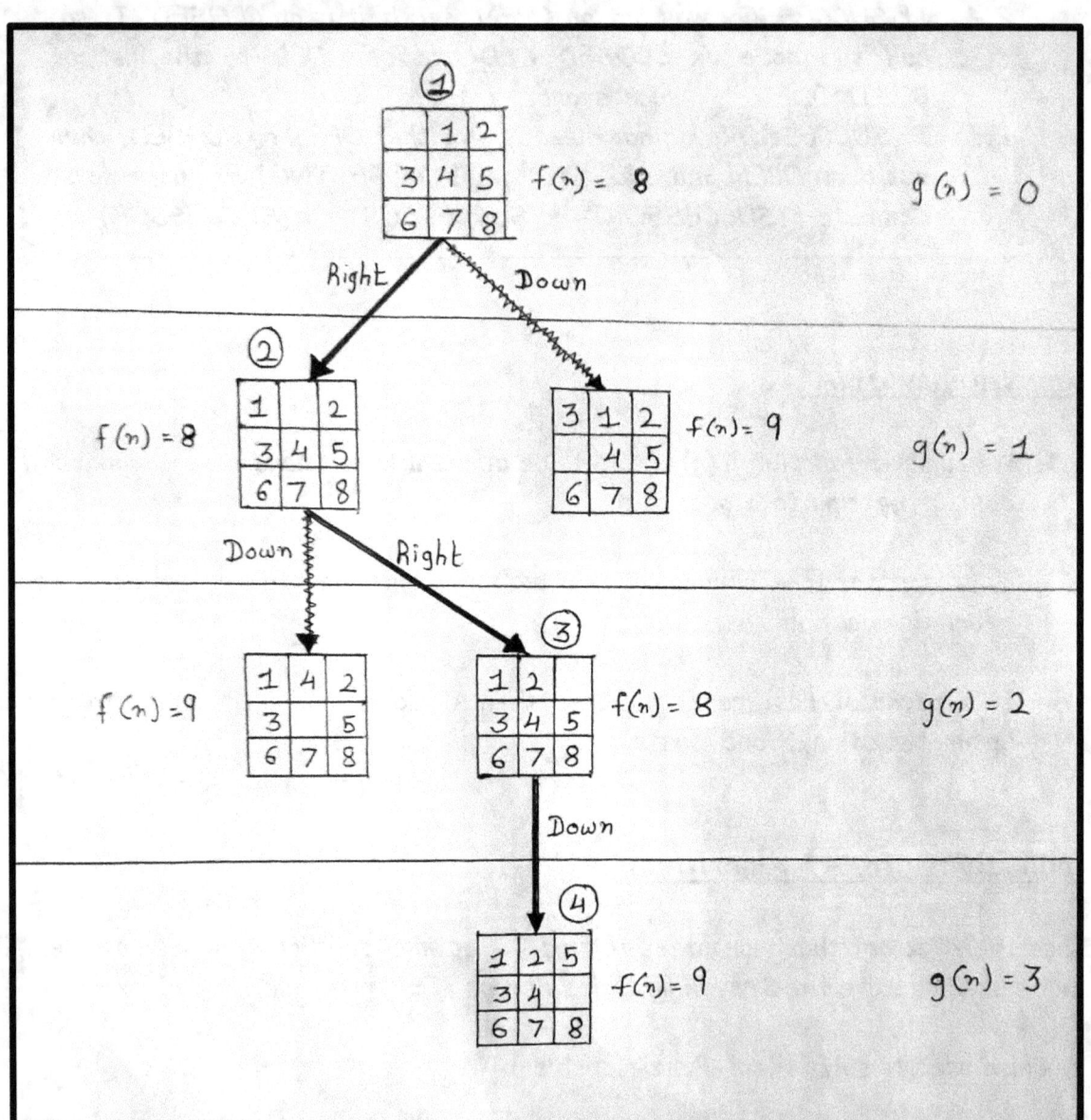

Figure 2.17: 8-Puzzle Problem - A* Algorithm - Example 1

The **heuristic function** applied to states in the above 8-puzzle problem is as follows:

f(n) = g(n) + h(n)

g(n) = actual distance from nth state to the start state
h(n) = number of tiles out of place

Example 2: Consider the following initial and goal configuration for 8-puzzle problem. Draw the search tree. Apply A* (Best First search) algorithm to reach from initial state to goal state and show the solution. Consider Manhattan distance as a heuristic function (i.e. sum of the distance & the number of tiles are out of place).

Initial State

1	2	3
7	8	4
6		5

Goal State

1	2	3
8		4
7	6	5

The **heuristic function** applied to states in the above 8-puzzle problem is as follows:

f(n) = g(n) + h(n)
g(n) = actual distance from nth state to the start state
h(n) = number of tiles out of place

Please Turn Over

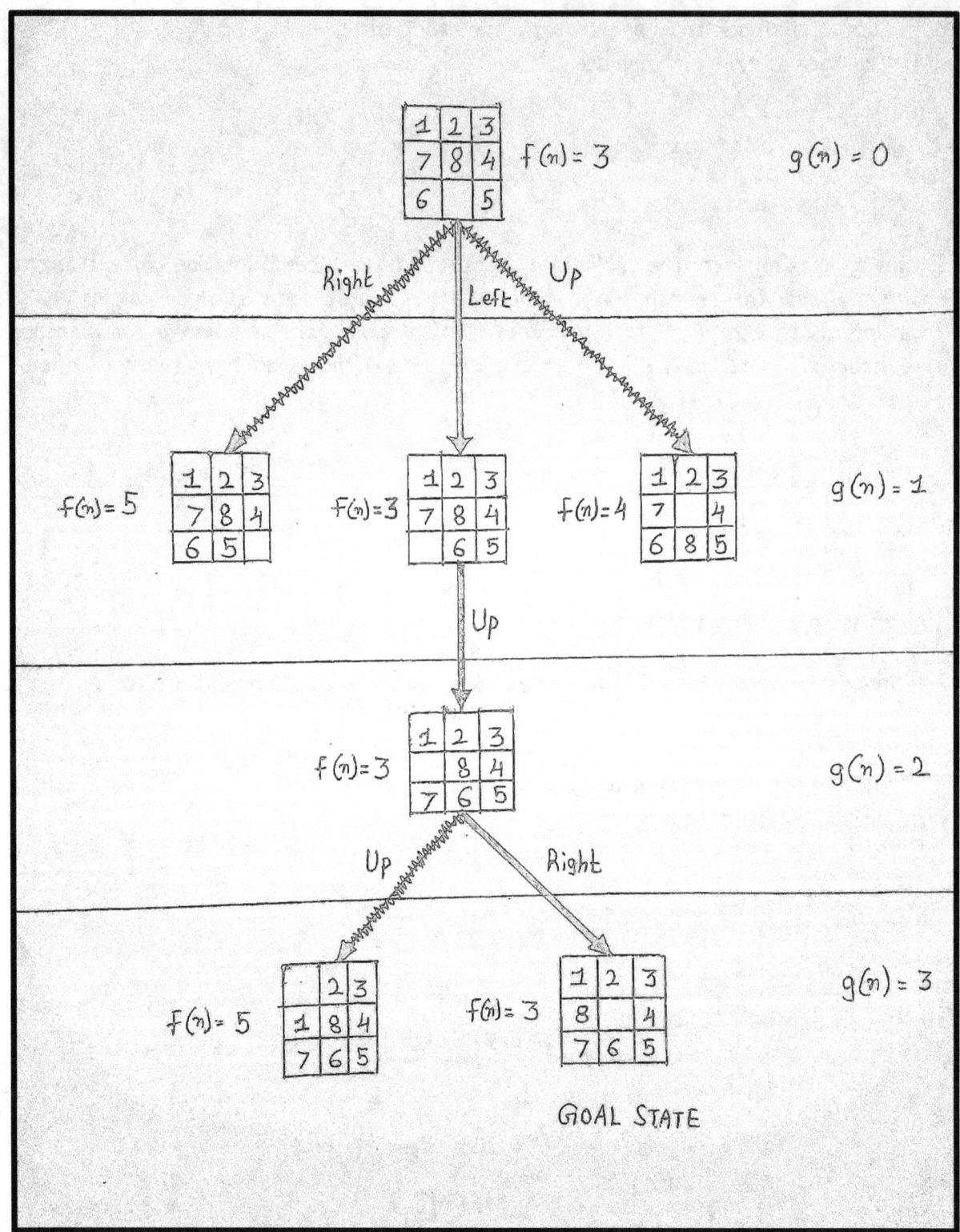

Figure 2.18: 8-Puzzle Problem - A* Algorithm - Example 2

2.8.4 Problem Reduction:

2.8.4.1 AND-OR Graphs:

AND-OR graph is useful for representing the **solution of problems that can be solved by decomposing them into a set of smaller problems**, all of which must then be solved. This **decomposition or reduction** generates arcs that we call **AND arcs**. Following is a simple **example of AND-OR graph:**

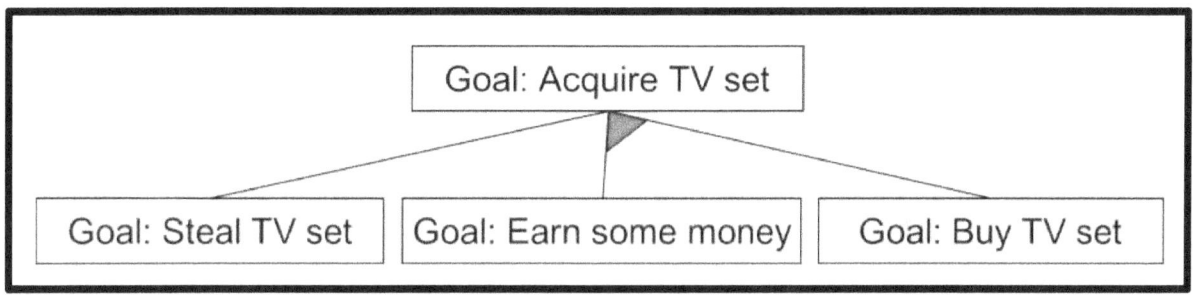

Figure 2.19: AND-OR Graph

The above graph divides the task of **acquiring TV set** in to two parts:

- **Steal TV Set**
- **Earn Some Money & Buy TV Set**

In order to find solutions in an **AND-OR graph**, we need an algorithm similar to **best-first search** but **with the ability to handle the AND arcs** appropriately.

In order to describe an algorithm for searching an **AND-OR graph**, we need to exploit a value that we call **FUTILITY**. If the estimated cost of a solution becomes greater than the value of **FUTILITY**, then we abandon the search. **FUTILITY** should be chosen to correspond to a **threshold** such that any solution with a cost above it is too expensive to be practical.

We use **AO* algorithm** to search an **AND-OR graph**.

2.8.4.2   AO* Algorithm:

Rather than the two lists, **OPEN & CLOSED**, that were used in the **A* algorithm**, the **AO* algorithm** will use a **single structure GRAPH**, representing the part of the search graph that has been explicitly generated so far. **Each node in the graph** will point both down to its **immediate successors** & up to its **immediate predecessors**.

AO* Algorithm:

1. Let GRAPH consist only of the node representing the initial state. Call this node INIT, Compute INIT.
2. Until INIT is labeled SOLVED or until INIT's h' value becomes greater than FUTILITY, repeat the following procedure:

   2.1. Trace the labeled arcs from INIT and select one of the unexpanded nodes, that occurs on this path, for expansion. Call the selected node as NODE.

   2.2. Generate the successors of NODE. If there are none, then assign FUTILITY as the h' value of NODE. This is equivalent to saying that NODE is not solvable. If there are successors, then for each one (called SUCCESSOR) that is not also an ancestor of NODE do the following:

   2.2.1.   Add SUCCESSOR to GRAPH
   2.2.2.   If SUCCESSOR is a terminal node, label it SOLVED and assign it an h' value of 0
   2.2.3.   If SUCCESSOR is not a terminal node, compute its h' value

   2.3. Propagate the newly discovered information up the graph by doing the following: Let S be a set of nodes that have been labeled SOLVED or whose h' values have been changed and so need to have values propagated back to their parents. Initialize S to NODE. Until S is empty, repeat the, following procedure:

2.3.1. If possible, select a node from S whose descendants in GRAPH doesn't occur in S. If there is no such node, select any node from S. Call this node CURRENT, and remove it from S.

2.3.2. Compute the cost of each of the arcs emerging from CURRENT. The cost of each arc is equal to the sum of the h' values of each of the nodes at the end of the arc plus whatever the cost of the arc itself is. Assign as CURRENT'S new h' value the minimum of the costs just computed for the arcs emerging from it.

2.3.3. Mark the best path out of CURRENT by marking the arc that had the minimum cost as computed in the previous step.

2.3.4. Mark CURRENT SOLVED if all of the nodes connected to it through the new labeled arc have been labeled SOLVED.

2.3.5. If CURRENT has been labeled SOLVED or if the cost of CURRENT was just changed, then its new status must be propagated back up the graph. So, add all of the ancestors of CURRENT to S.

2.8.5 Constraint Satisfaction:

This method is used to solve the problems in which the goal is to discover some problem state that satisfies a given set of constraints. Examples of this sort of problem include cryptarithmetic puzzles.

Constraint satisfaction is a search procedure that operates in a space of constraint sets. The initial state contains the constraints that are originally given in the problem description. A Goal State is any state that has been completely constrained. For example, for cryptarithmetic puzzle, completely constrained means that each letter has been assigned a unique numeric value.

Constraint satisfaction is a two-step process. First, constraints are discovered and propagated throughout the system. Then, if there is still not a solution, search begins.

Algorithm for **Constraint Satisfaction** is as follows:

> 1. Propagate available constraints. To do this first detect all the objects that must have values assigned to them in a complete solution. Now add all the detected objects to OPEN. Then do until an inconsistency is detected or until OPEN is empty:
>
>   1.1. Select an object OB from OPEN. Strengthen as much as possible the set of constraints that apply to OB.
>   1.2. If this set is different from the set that was assigned the last time OB was examined or if this is the first-time OB has been examined, then add to OPEN all objects that share any constraints with OB.
>   1.3. Remove OB from OPEN.
>
> 2. If the union of the constraints discovered above defines a solution, then quit and report the solution.
> 3. If the union of the constraints discovered above defines a contradiction, then return the failure.

4. If neither of the above occurs, then it is necessary to make a guess at something in order to proceed. To do this loop until a solution is found or all possible solutions have been eliminated:

   4.1. Select an object whose value is not yet determined and select a way of strengthening the constraints on that object.
   4.2. Recursively invoke constraint satisfaction with the current set of constraints augmented by strengthening constraint just selected.

2.8.6 Means-Ends Analysis:

So far, we have presented a collection of search strategies that can reason either forward or backward. Often, a mixture of the two directions is appropriate. Such a mixed strategy would make it possible to solve the major parts of a problem first and then go back and solve the small problems that arise in "gluing" the big pieces together. A technique known as means-ends analysis allows us to do that.

The means-ends analysis process centers around the detection of differences between the current state and the goal state. Once such a difference is isolated, an operator that can reduce the difference must be found. If the operator cannot be applied to the current state, we set up a sub-problem of getting to a state in which it can be applied.

Algorithm: Means-Ends Analysis

1. Compare CURRENT to GOAL. If there are no differences between them then return.

2. Otherwise, select the most important difference and reduce it by doing the following until success or failure is signaled:

    2.1. Select an untried operator O that is applicable to the current difference. If there are no such operators, then signal failure.

    2.2. Attempt to apply O to CURRENT. Generate descriptions of two states: OSTART, a state in which O's preconditions are satisfied & ORESULT, the state that would result if O were applied in O-START.

    2.3. If (FIRST-PART ← MEA (CURRENT, O-START)) & (LAST-PART ← MEA (O-RESULT, GOAL)) are successful, then signal success and return the result of concatenating FIRST-PART, O, and LAST-PART.

2.9 Examples: Cryptarithmetic Problems

Goal State:
All letters have been assigned a digit in such a way that all the initial constraints are satisfied.

Constraints:
No two letters have the same value.
The sums of the digits must be as shown in the problem.

Example 1: SEND-MORE-MONEY

Solve the following Cryptarithmetic problem:

```
  S E N D
+ M O R E
---------
M O N E Y
```

- Initial guess, M=1 because the sum of two single digits can generate at most a carry of '1'.

- If M=1, then S should be either 8 or 9 because S + M gives a two-digit number. This also considers the carry digit.

- When M=1 & S=8/9, the two-digit result of M+S can either be 10 or 11. That is, O will be either 0 or 1. But, 1 is already assigned to M so it can't be assigned to any other digit. Thus, O=0, (M + S) = 10. S can be 8/9 depending on the carry.

- Now, E+O=N, which is only possible if there's a carry of 1 because otherwise, E+O=E. Thus, N=E+1 & C2=1.

- So far, we have M=1, S=8/9, O=0, C2=1. We're struck here because we don't know the value of E. Thus, we'll try different possible values of E.

- For E=5, N=6, (N+R) = 15, R = 8/9. (D+2) = Y. Again, we don't know the value of C1. Son, we'll assume it.

➤ For C1 = 1, R = 8, S = 9, (D+5) = 10+Y. Maximum value of D can be 7. If D=7, Y=2.

➤ So, M=1, S=9, O=0, E=5, N=6, R=8, D=7, E=5, Y=2

Thus, we have our probable solution as follows:

```
  SEND           9567
 +MORE          +1085
 ------         -----
 MONEY          10652
```

Example 2: EAT-THAT-APPLE

Solve the following Cryptarithmetic problem:

```
    E A T
 + T H A T
 ---------
  A P P L E
```

- Initial guess, A = 1, because the sum of two single digits can generate at most a carry of '1'.

- T = 9 & C3 = 1.

- Thus, P = 0. E + H = 10, C2 = 0.

- A=1. Thus, A+A = L = 2/3.

- We have T=9. Thus, T + T = 18. Thus, E = 8, C1 = 1 & L = 3.

- E + H = 10. Thus, H = 2.

Thus, we have our probable solution as follows:

```
    E A T              8 1 9
 + T H A T          + 9 2 1 9
 ---------          ---------
  A P P L E          1 0 0 3 8
```

Example 3: BASE-BALL-GAMES

Solve the following Cryptarithmetic problem:

```
  B A S E
+ B A L L
---------
G A M E S
```

- Initial guess, G = 1, because the sum of two single digits can generate at most a carry of '1'.

- Now, B+B+C3 >= 10. Thus, B >= 5. Value of B can't be 5 because if B = 5, A will be 0 & if A will be 0 the M will either be 1 or 0, which is not possible because those two values are already assigned. Thus, possible values of B are 6,7,8,9.

- Let us assume that C3 = 0 & B = 7. Then, A = 4 & M = 8/9 (depending on the carry).

- Now, the characters remaining are E, L, S & the values remaining are 0,2,3,5,6,8/9.

- Assume L = 5 & E = 3. Thus, S = 8. This generates a carry, C2 = 1. Thus, M = 9.

Thus, we have our probable solution as follows:

```
  B A S E         7 4 8 3
+ B A L L       + 7 4 5 5
---------       ---------
G A M E S        1 4 9 3 8
```

Artificial Intelligence

Example 4: DONALD-GERALD-ROBERT

Solve the following Cryptarithmetic problem:

```
  DONALD
+ GERALD
--------
  ROBERT
```

- Initial guess, T is even (D + D) (Sum of two numbers is always Even). Possible values of T are 0,2,4,6,8

- Let's assume that D=5. Thus, T=0 & C_1=1. This implies that R is odd. Possible values of R are 1,3,7,9 (5 is already assigned).

- O + E + C_4 = O.
  E can't be 0 because 0 is already assigned to T.
  Thus, E + C_4 = 10 & C_4 = 1.
  Thus, E = 9 & C_5 = 1.

- E = 9 so that C_2 = 1.
  A + A + 1 = E
  2A = 9 – 1
  A = 4

- L >= 5. Possible values of L = 6 or 8. We can't use 7 because 7+7+1=15 & 5 is already assigned to D (R can't be 5). We also can't use 5 & 9 because they are already assigned to D & E.

- Possible values of R = 3 or 7.

- Let's assume the value of L = 6. This implies R = 3.

  Now, D + G + C_5 = R
  5 + G + 1 = 3

  This is NOT POSSIBLE. Thus, VALUE OF L CAN NOT BE 6.

- Let's again assume the value of L = 8. This implies R = 7.

Now, D + G + C5 = R
5 + G + 1 = 7
G = 1

> Remaining Characters: R, N, B, O

Remaining Values: 2, 3, 6

Also,
R + N = 10 + B
7 + N = 10 + B
N = 3 + B

Thus, N = 6, B = 3 & O = 2

Thus, we have our probable solution as follows:

```
   DONALD          5 2 6 4 8 5
 + GERALD         +1 9 7 4 8 5
 -------------    ----------------
   ROBERT          7 2 3 9 7 0
```

Example 5: CROSS-ROADS-DANGER

Solve the following Cryptarithmetic problem:

```
  C R O S S
+ R O A D S
---------------
D A N G E R
```

- Initial guess, D = 1, because the sum of two single digits can generate at most a carry of '1'.

- Now, S + S = R = Even (sum of two same numbers is always even).

- Let S = 3. This implies, R = 6 & C1 = 0.

- E = S + D + C1
  E = 3 + 1 + 0
  E = 4 & C2 = 0

- C + R + C4 = 10 + A
C + 6 + C4 = 10 + A

Let C4 = 0

C = 4 + A
C > 3

C = 5 or 7 or 8 or 9

- 10 + A = C + R + C4
10 + A = C + 6 + 0
A = C - 4

If C = 5, A = 1. This isn't possible because 1 is already assigned.
If C = 7, A = 6. This isn't possible because 6 is already assigned.
If C = 8, A = 4. This isn't possible because 4 is already assigned.

Thus, C = 9. This implies, A = 5.

➢ Remaining characters: O, G, N
Remaining values: 0, 2, 7, 8, 9

Also,
O + A + C2 = G
O + 5 + 0 = G
O + 5 = G

Thus, O = 2, G = 7 & C3 = 0.

➢ N = R + O + C3
N = 6 + 2 + 0
N = 8

Thus, we have our probable solution as follows:

```
  C R O S S              9 6 2 3 3
+ R O A D S            + 6 2 5 1 3
---------------        ---------------
D A N G E R              1 5 8 7 4 6
```

Chapter 3

Knowledge Representation Issues

3.1 Representations & Mappings:

In order to solve the complex problems encountered in AI, one needs both a **large amount of knowledge (facts)** & **some mechanisms for manipulating that knowledge** to create solutions. Consider the following before discussing about knowledge representations & mapping:

- **Facts**: truths in some relevant world. These are the things we want to represent.
- **Representations of facts** in some chosen format. These are the things we will actually be able to manipulate.

Mapping between facts & representations can be structured at **two levels**: **The knowledge level**, at which facts are described, & **the symbol level**, at which representations of objects at the knowledge level are defined in terms of symbols that can be manipulated.

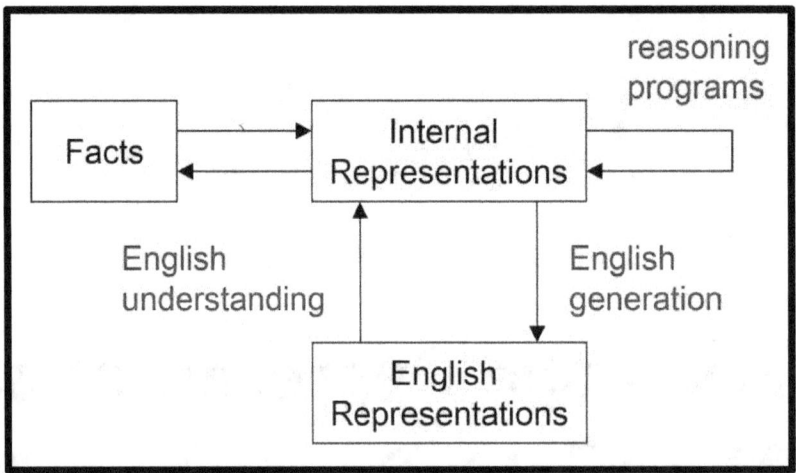

Figure 3.1: Mapping between Facts & Representations

Let's look at a **simple example** using mathematical logic as the representational format. Consider the English sentences:

Spot is a dog.
Every dog has a tail.

The facts represented by these English sentences can be represented in logic as follows:

> **dog (Spot)**   // Spot is a dog.
> **∀x: dog (x) → hastail (x)**   // Every dog has a tail.
>
> From the above two logic representations, we can derive that Spot has tail & represent it in logic as follows:
>
> **hastail (Spot)**   // Spot has tail
>
> Using an appropriate backward mapping function, we could then generate the English sentence for the resultant logic.

Logical representation of facts is necessary because a machine can easily manipulate logical representation of facts rather than the English representation.

Representing English facts in the form of logic can be termed as <u>**Forward Representation Mapping**</u>.

Representing the logic in the form of English facts can be termed as <u>**Backward Representation Mapping**</u>.

Converting the initial facts in the final facts can be termed as <u>**Reasoning**</u>.

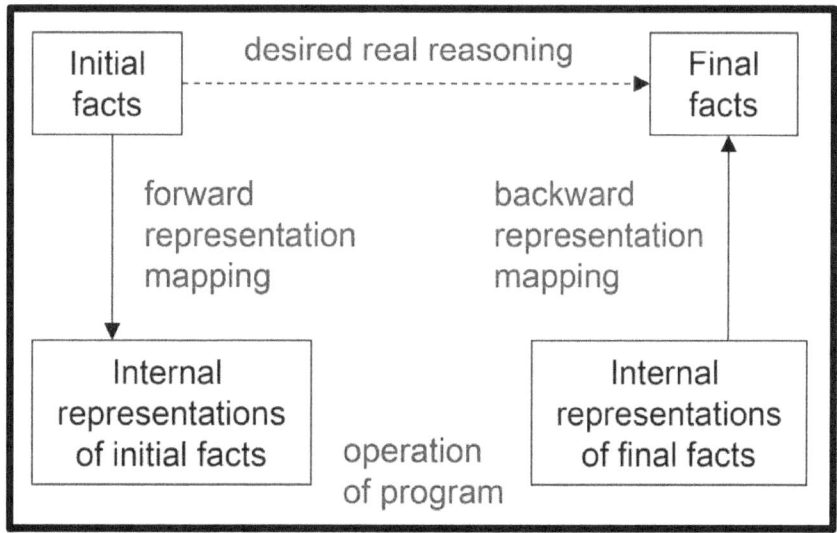

Figure 3.2: Representation of Facts

3.2 Approaches to Knowledge Representation:

A *good system for the representation of knowledge* should possess the following *four properties*:

I. **Representational Adequacy**: Ability to represent all kinds of knowledge that are needed in the domain.

II. **Inferential Adequacy**: Ability to manipulate representational structures such that new knowledge can be derived / inferred from the old.

III. **Inferential Efficiency**: Ability to incorporate additional information into an existing knowledge base that can be used to drive inference mechanisms in the most promising direction.

IV. **Acquisitional Efficiency**: Ability to easily acquire new information.

Unfortunately, no such system exist that optimizes all of the capabilities for all kinds of knowledge. As a result, multiple techniques for knowledge representation exist. The most important of these techniques are described in the following section:

1. Simple Relational Knowledge:

The simplest way to represent declarative facts is as a set of relations of the same sort used in database systems. Example:

Player	Height	Weight	Handed
Peter	6-0	180	Right
John	6-2	215	Left
Ricky	6-3	205	Right

This kind of knowledge representation provides very weak inferential capabilities but knowledge represented in this form may serve as the input to more powerful inference engines.

For example, the above example fails to infer that which player can face which kind of bowler.

2. Inheritable knowledge:

Here the knowledge elements are organized into classes and classes are organized in a generalization hierarchy. This hierarchy facilitates the elements of specific classes to inherit attributes and values from other classes. Example:

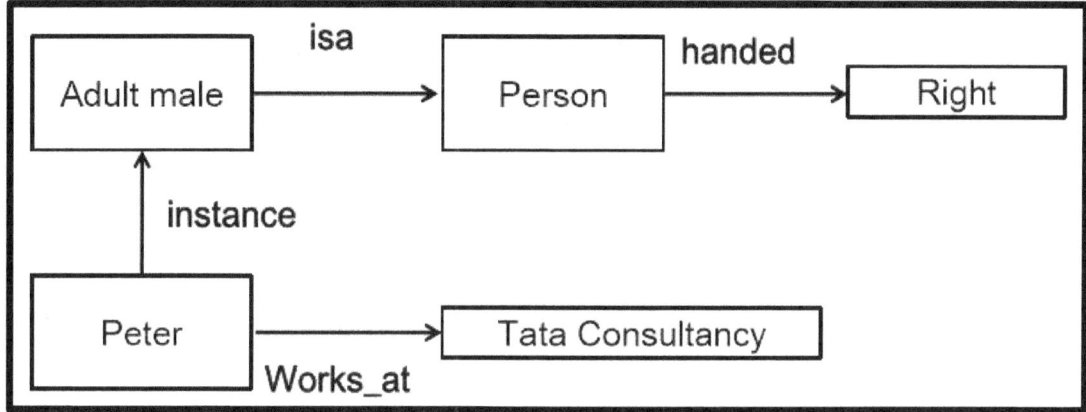

Figure 3.3: Inheritable Knowledge Representation

The inheritance is a powerful form of inference, but not adequate.

3. *Inferential knowledge*:

Here, the facts are represented in a logical form, which facilitates reasoning. Example:

1. "Marcus is a man"
2. "All men are mortal"

Implies: "Marcus is mortal"

An inference engine is required in this kind of knowledge representation.

4. *Procedural knowledge*:

Here, the control information, required to use the knowledge, is embedded in the knowledge itself. For example, computer programs. Knowledge is encoded in some small programs that know how to do specific things & proceed.

3.3 Declarative versus Procedural Representation of Knowledge:

Sr. No.	Declarative Representation	Procedural Representation
1	Declarative knowledge is defined as the factual information which is stored in memory and also it is known to be static in nature.	The procedural knowledge is generally a compiled or a processed form of the information. It is related to the performance of some task.
2	Declarative knowledge involves knowing that something is the case.	Procedural knowledge involves knowing how to do something.
3	For example: B is the second letter of the English alphabet.	For example: a computer program to carry out a specific task.
4	Higher level of abstraction.	Lower level of abstraction.
5	Good modifiability & readability.	Poor modifiability & readability.
6	Poor computational efficiency.	Good computational efficiency.
7	Better for end-users.	Better for knowledge engineers.
8	It is also known as descriptive knowledge & propositional knowledge.	---

3.4 Issues in Knowledge Representation:

The issues that arise while using Knowledge Representation techniques are as follows:

1. Important Attributes:

Are any attributes of objects so basic that they occur in almost every problem domain? If such attributes exist, what are they?

There are two attributes that are of very general significance: **INSTANCE** & **ISA**. These attributes are important because they support property inheritance.

2. Relationship among Attributes:

Are there any important relationships that exist among attributes of objects?

The attributes that we use to describe objects have the following four properties independent of the knowledge they encode:

- *Inverses* (binary relationships)
- *Existence in an ISA hierarchy* (generalization-specialization)
- *Techniques for reasoning* (inferring unknown values)
- *Single valued attributes* (handling attributes with unique values)

3. Choosing Granularity:

At what level should knowledge be represented?

High-level facts may not be adequate for inference. Low-level primitives may require a lot of storage.

Ex: "john spotted sue"

Representation: spotted (agent(john), object(sue))

Q1: "who spotted sue?"   Ans1: "john".

Q2: "Did john see sue?"   Ans2: NO ANSWER

Add detailed fact: spotted (x, y) → saw (x, y)
Now, Ans2: "Yes"

4. Set of Objects:

How should sets of objects be represented?

There are certain properties of objects that are true as member of a set but not as individual; Thus, set of objects should be represented keeping that in mind.

5. Finding Right Structure:

Given a large amount of knowledge stored in a database, how can relevant parts be accessed when they are needed?

This is about access to right structure for describing a particular situation. This requires selecting an initial structure & then revising the choice. While doing so, it is necessary to address the problems like: how to perform an initial selection of the most appropriate structure, how to fill in appropriate details from the current situations, how to find a better structure if the one chosen initially turns out to be inappropriate, what to do if none of the available structures is appropriate, when to create and remember a new structure & so on.

3.5 The Frame Problem:

In the confined world of a robot, surroundings are not static. Many varying forces or actions can cause changes or modifications to the surroundings. The problem of forcing a robot to adapt to these changes is the basis of the **frame problem** in artificial intelligence. Information in the knowledge base & the robot's conclusions combine to decide what the robot's subsequent action should be.

A good selection from the facts can be made by discarding or ignoring irrelevant facts that could have negative side effects. A robot must introduce facts that are relevant to a particular moment. That is, a robot will examine its current situation, and then look up the facts that will be beneficial to choosing its subsequent action. This whole problem of representing the facts that change as well as those that do not is known as the **frame problem**.

3.6 Expert System:

An **expert system** is an **interactive computer-based decision tool** that uses both facts & heuristics to **solve difficult decision making problems**, based on **knowledge acquired from an expert**.

> Inference engine + Knowledge = Expert system

Expert systems are **computer applications** which represent some **non-algorithmic expertise** for solving certain **types of problems**. For example:

- Diagnostic applications
- Play chess
- Make financial planning decisions
- Configure computers
- Monitor real time systems
- Underwrite insurance policies

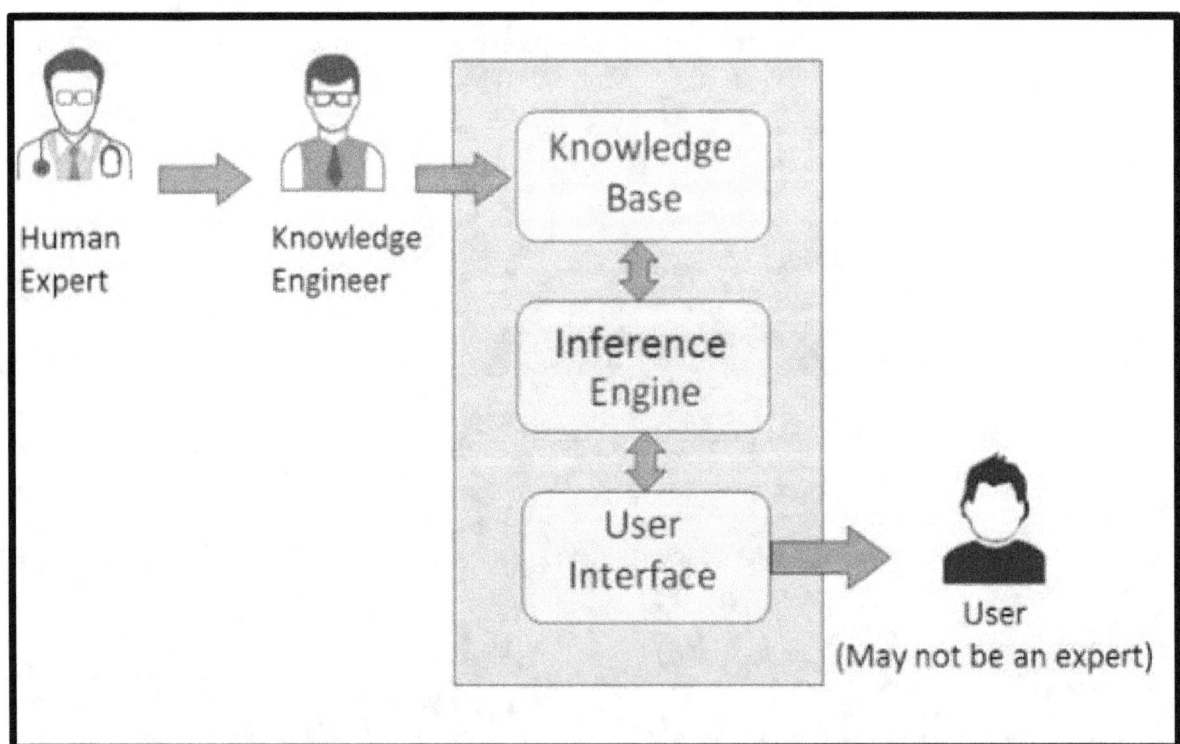

Figure 3.4: Components of an Expert System

Major components of an expert system are: Knowledge Base, Inference Engine & User Interface.

- **_Knowledge Base_**: The knowledge base contains the knowledge necessary for understanding, formulating, and solving problems. The success of any expert system (ES) majorly depends upon the collection of accurate and precise knowledge.

- **_Inference Engine_**: It's the brain of the ES. It uses efficient procedures and rules to deduce a correct & flawless solution. In case of knowledge-based ES, the Inference Engine acquires and manipulates the knowledge from the knowledge base to arrive at a particular solution.

- **_User Interface_**: User interface provides interaction between the ES & the user of the ES. It is generally Natural Language Processing so as to be used by the user who is not necessarily an expert in Artificial Intelligence.

3.6.1 *Knowledge Acquisition*:

Knowledge acquisition is the process of adding new knowledge to a knowledge base & refining / improving the knowledge that already exists. Acquisition is usually associated with some purpose such as expanding the capabilities of a system or improving its performance at some specified task. It is goal oriented creation and refinement of knowledge.

The success of knowledge based expert systems lies in the quality & extent of the knowledge available to the system. Acquiring and validating a large amount of consistent & correlated knowledge is big problem. This has given the acquisition process an especially important role in the design and implementation of these systems. Consequently, effective acquisition methods have become one of the principal challenges for the AI researchers.

The goal of knowledge acquisition is the discovery & development of efficient, cost effective methods of acquisition.

3.6.2 Expert System Shell:

Many expert systems are built with products called **expert system shells (ESS)**. A shell is *a **piece of software*** which contains the ***user interface, a format for declarative knowledge in the knowledge base, & an inference engine***. The knowledge and system engineers uses these shells in making **expert systems (ES)**.

Knowledge engineer uses the shell to build a system for a particular problem domain.

System engineer builds the user interface, designs the declarative format of the knowledge base, and implements the inference engine.

Chapter 4

Using Predicate Logic

4.1 Introduction to Logic:

The *logical representation* of a language is useful because a machine can easily use it to derive new knowledge from existing knowledge using **mathematical deduction**.

Proposition: A proposition is a **simple declarative sentence**. For example, *"the book is expensive"* is a proposition. A proposition can be either **true or false**.

Propositional Logic: Propositional logic is a simple language used for **representation of key ideas & definitions**. It comprises of **logical constants (true & false), user defined propositional symbols (P, Q, R, S, ...), & connectives** that are used to combine the propositions. Some of the **commonly used connectives** are:

∧	and	[conjunction]
∨	or	[disjunction]
⇒	implies	[implication]
¬	not	[negation]
∀	For all	
∃	There exists	

In propositional logic, real world facts can be represented by **Well-Formed Formulas (WFFs)**. An **example of WFF** is as follows:

If S and T are sentences, then (S ∧ T), (S ∨ T), (S → T), and (S ↔ T) are sentences.

4.2 Representing Simple Facts in Logic:

The *propositional logic* is *not powerful enough* to represent all types of assertions that are used in AI, or to express certain types of relationship between propositions such as equivalence. For example, the assertion "x is greater than 1" is not a proposition because you can't tell whether it is true or false unless you know the value of x.

Thus, we need *more powerful logic* to deal with these kinds of problems. The *first-order predicate logic* (or just *predicate logic*) is one of such logic.

Consider the following *example* that shows the use of predicate logic as a way of representing knowledge:

1. Marcus was a man.
2. Marcus was a Pompeian.
3. All Pompeiians were Romans.
4. Caesar was a ruler.
5. All Pompeiians were either loyal to Caesar or hated him.
6. Everyone is loyal to someone.
7. People only try to assassinate rulers they are not loyal to.
8. Marcus tried to assassinate Caesar.

The facts described by the above sentences can be represented as a set of *well-formed formulas (WFFs)* as follows:

1. Marcus was a man.
man(Marcus)

2. Marcus was a Pompeian.
Pompeian(Marcus)

3. All Pompeiians were Romans.
∀x: Pompeian(x) → Roman(x)

4. Caesar was a ruler.
ruler(Caesar)

5. All Pompeiians were either loyal to Caesar or hated him.
   inclusive-or
   $\forall x: Roman(x) \rightarrow loyalto(x, Caesar) \lor hate(x, Caesar)$
   exclusive-or
   $\forall x: Roman(x) \rightarrow (loyalto(x, Caesar) \land \neg hate(x, Caesar)) \lor (\neg loyalto(x, Caesar) \land hate(x, Caesar))$

6. Every-one is loyal to someone.
   $\forall x: \exists y: loyalto(x, y)$

7. People only try to assassinate rulers they are not loyal to.
   $\forall x: \forall y: person(x) \land ruler(y) \land tryassassinate(x, y) \rightarrow \neg loyalto(x, y)$

8. Marcus tried to assassinate Caesar.
   tryassassinate (Marcus, Caesar)

Now suppose if we want to use these statements to answer the question:
Was Marcus loyal to Caesar?

> man(Marcus) [1]
> ruler(Caesar) [4]
> tryassassinate (Marcus, Caesar) [8]
> person(Marcus) ∧ ruler(Caesar) ∧ tryassassinate (Marcus, Caesar)
> ↓
> ¬loyalto (Marcus, Caesar) [7]

Thus, Marcus was not loyal to Caesar.

4.3 Representing Instance & ISA Relationships:

The attributes **Instance** & **ISA** play important role in a useful form of reasoning called **property inheritance**.

The following figure shows the first five sentences of the previous example **represented in logic in three different ways**:

---
1. Man(Marcus).
2. Pompeian(Marcus).
3. ∀x: Pompeian(x) → Roman(x).
4. ruler(Caesar).
5. ∀x: Roman(x) → loyalto(x, Caesar) ∨ hate(x, Caesar).

---
1. instance(Marcus, man).
2. instance(Marcus, Pompeian).
3. ∀x: instance(x, Pompeian) → instance(x, Roman).
4. instance(Caesar, ruler).
5. ∀x: instance(x, Roman). → loyalto(x, Caesar) ∨ hate(x, Caesar).

---
1. instance(Marcus, man).
2. instance(Marcus, Pompeian).
3. isa(Pompeian, Roman)
4. instance(Caesar, ruler).
5. ∀x: instance(x, Roman). → loyalto(x, Caesar) ∨ hate(x, Caesar).
6. ∀x: ∀y: ∀z: instance(x, y) ∧ isa(y, z) → instance(x, z).

Figure 4.1: Three Ways of Representing Class Membership

The **first part** of the figure contains the representations that we discussed in the previous example. In these representations, **class membership is represented with unary predicates** (such as Roman), each of which corresponds to a class. Asserting that P(x) is true is equivalent to asserting that x is an instance of class P.

The **_second part_** of the figure contains representations that **_use the instance predicate explicitly_**. The **_predicate instance is a binary one_**, whose first argument is an object & whose second argument is a class to which the object belongs. However, these representations do not use an explicit ISA predicate. Instead they describe subclass relationships as shown in axiom 3 (the one between Pompeian & Roman). This rule states that if an object is an instance of the subclass Pompeian then it is an instance of the superclass Roman.

The **_third part_** contains representations that **_uses both the Instance & ISA predicates explicitly_**. The use of the ISA predicate simplifies the representation of sentence 3 but it requires one additional axiom (shown here as number 6).

4.4 Computable Functions & Predicates:

In the example that we explored in the previous section, all the simple facts were expressed as combinations of individual predicates. This is fine if the number of facts is not very large. But if we want to express facts like the following greater-than and less-than relationships:

$$\begin{array}{ll} gt\,(1,\,0) & lt\,(0,\,1) \\ gt\,(2,\,1) & lt\,(1,\,2) \\ gt\,(3,\,2) & lt\,(2,\,3) \end{array}$$

Clearly, we do not want to write the representation of each of these facts individually. For one thing, there are infinitely many of them. But even if we only consider the finite number of them, it would be extremely inefficient to store explicitly a large set of statements. Instead, we could easily compute each one of it as we need them. For doing so, we need to have computable predicates.

For an instance, if we want to compute the truth of gt (2 + 3, 1), we first need to compute the value of the plus function given the arguments 2 and 3, and then send the arguments 5 and 1 to gt function.

4.5 Resolution:

Resolution is a procedure that is used to **prove/disprove some statement** by **operating on the existing statements** that have been converted to a very convenient standard form.

Resolution produces proofs by **refutation**. In other words, to prove a statement, resolution attempts to show that the negation of the statement produces a contradiction with the known statements.

The **resolution** procedure is a **simple iterative process**: At each step, two clauses, called the **parent clauses, are compared (resolved), resulting into a new clause** that has been inferred from them.

The new clause represents ways that the two parent clauses interact with each other. Suppose that there are two clauses in the system:

winter V summer
¬ winter V cold

Now we observe that precisely one of **winter & ¬ winter** will be true at any point. If **winter is true, then cold must be true** to guarantee the truth of the second clause. If **¬ winter is true, then summer must be true** to guarantee the truth of the first clause. Thus, we see that from these two clauses we can deduce:

summer V cold

This is the deduction that the resolution procedure will make. Resolution operates by taking two clauses that each contains the same literal, in this example, winter. The **literal must occur in positive form in one clause & in negative form in the other.** The **new clause** is obtained by **combining all of the literals of the two parent clauses except the ones that cancel.**

If the clause that is produced is the empty clause, then a contradiction has been found. For example, the two clauses: **winter & ¬ winter will produce the empty clause.**

4.5.1 Conversion to Clause Form:

To apply resolution, we need to **reduce a set of Well-Formed Formulas (WFFs) to a set of clauses**, where a **clause is defined to be a WFF in conjunctive normal form but with no instances of the connector.**

To **convert a WFF into clause form**, perform the following **sequence of steps**:

1. *Eliminate* → *operator*, using the fact that $a → b$ is equivalent to ¬ a V b.

2. **Reduce the scope of each ¬ to a single term**, using the fact that ¬ (¬ p) = p.

3. **Standardize variables so that each quantifier binds a unique variable.** Since variables are just dummy names, this process cannot affect the truth value of the WFF.

   <u>Example</u>, ∀x: P(x) V ∀x: Q(x) will be converted to ∀x: P(x) V ∀y: Q(y)

4. **Move all quantifiers to the left of the formula** without changing their relative order. This is possible since there is no conflict among variable names.

5. **Eliminate existential quantifiers**. This can be done by introducing **Skolem functions**.

   <u>Example</u>: If we convert ∃y: President(y) in to President(S1)
   ∀x: ∃y: father-of (y, x) will be converted to ∀x: father-of (S2(x), x)

   where, **S2(x)** is a **Skolem function** which gives the value of the existential quantifier that previously existed.

6. **Drop the prefix**. At this point, **all remaining variables are universally quantified**, so the prefix can just be dropped.

   <u>Example</u>: ∀x: [¬ Roman (x) V ¬ know (x, Marcus)]
   will be converted to
   ¬ Roman (x) V ¬ know (x, Marcus)

7. **Convert the matrix into a conjunction of disjuncts** (*remove the parenthesis*).

   <u>Example</u>: (a ∧ b) V c = (a V c) ∧ (b V c)

8. **Create a separate clause corresponding to each conjunct.** In order for a **WFF to be true, all the clauses** that are generated from it **must be true**.

9. **Rename the variables so that no two clauses make reference to the same variable.** In making this transformation, we rely on the fact that:

   $(\forall x: P(x) \land Q(x)) = \forall x: P(x) \land \forall x: Q(x)$

Since **each clause is a separate conjunct** & since **all the variables are universally quantified**, there need be **no relationship between the variables of two clauses, even if they were generated from the same WFF**.

4.5.2 Propositional Resolution:

In order to make it clear how resolution works, we first present **the resolution procedure for propositional logic**. We then expand it to include predicate logic in the later section.

In propositional logic, the procedure for **producing a proof** for the **proposition P** with respect to a **given set of axioms F** is the following:

1. **Convert all the propositions of F to clause form.**
2. **Negate P & convert the result to clause form**. Add it to the set of clauses obtained in step 1.
3. Repeat until either **a contradiction is found or no progress can be made**:

   3.1. Select **two clauses**. Call these the **parent clauses**.
   3.2. **Resolve them together**. The **resulting clause**, called **the resolvent**, will be **the disjunction of all of the literals of both of the parent clauses** with the following exception: If there are any pairs of literals L & $\neg L$ such that **one of the parent clauses contains L & the other one contains $\neg L$**, then select one such pair and **eliminate both L & $\neg L$** from the resolvent.
   3.3. If the **resolvent is the empty clause, then a contradiction has been found**. If it is not, then add it to the set of clauses available to the procedure.

4.5.3 The Unification Algorithm:

In **propositional logic**, it is **easy to determine that two literals cannot both be true at the same time** by simply looking for **L & ¬ L**.

In **predicate logic**, this **matching process is more complicated** since the **arguments of the predicates must be considered**. For **example**, man (John) & ¬ man(John) is a contradiction, while man(John) & ¬ man(Spot) is not.

Thus, in order **to determine contradictions**, we need a **matching procedure** that **compares two literals & discovers whether there exists a set of substitutions that makes them identical**. There is a straightforward **recursive procedure**, called <u>the unification algorithm</u>, that does it.

In **unification algorithm**, each **literal is represented as a list**, where **first element** is the **name of a predicate** & the **remaining elements** are **arguments**. The **argument** may be a **single element** or may be **another list**. For example, we can have literals as

    (tryassassinate Marcus Caesar)
        OR
    (tryassassinate Marcus (ruler of Rome))

To **unify two literals**, first check if their **first elements are same. If so, proceed. Else, they can't be unified**. For example, the **following literals can't be unified**:

    (try assassinate Marcus Caesar)
        &
    (hate Marcus Caesar)

The **unification algorithm** recursively matches pairs of elements, one pair at a time. The **matching rules** are:

> ➢ **Different constants, functions or predicates can't match, whereas identical ones can.**

> ➢ **The substitution must be consistent.** Substituting y for x now & then z for x later is inconsistent.

> *A variable can match another variable, any constant or a function or predicate expression*, subject to the condition that *the function or predicate expression must not contain any instance of the variable being matched*.

Algorithm: Unify (A, B)

1. If A or B are both variables or constants, then:
    - 1.1. If A & B are identical, then return NIL.
    - 1.2. Else if A is a variable, then if A occurs in B then return {FAIL}, else return (B/A).
    - 1.3. Else if B is a variable, then if B occurs in A then return {FAIL}, else return (A/B).
    - 1.4. Else return {FAIL}.

2. If the initial predicate symbols in A & B are not identical, then return {FAIL}.
3. If A & B have a different number of arguments, then return {FAIL}.
4. Set SUBST to NIL. (At the end of this procedure, SUBST will contain all the substitutions used to unify A & B)

5. For i ← 1 to number of arguments in A:
    - 5.1. S = Unify (i^{th} argument of A, i^{th} argument of B).
    - 5.2. If S contains FAIL then return {FAIL}.
    - 5.3. If S is not equal to NIL then:
        - 5.3.1. Apply S to the remainder of both A & B.
        - 5.3.2. SUBST = APPEND (S, SUBST).

6. Return SUBST.

4.5.4 Predicate Logic Resolution:

In predicate logic, the procedure for **producing a proof** for the **statement P** with respect to a **given set of statements F** is the following:

Algorithm: Predicate Logic Resolution

1. **Convert all the statements of F to clause form.**
2. **Negate P & convert the result to clause form.** Add it to the set of clauses obtained in 1.
3. **Repeat until a contradiction is found, no progress can be made, or a predetermined amount of effort has been expended.**

    3.1. **Select two clauses.** Call these the **parent clauses**.

    3.2. **Resolve them together. The resolvent** will be the **disjunction of all the literals of both parent clauses** with appropriate substitutions performed & with the **following exception**: If there is one pair of literals **T1 & ¬T2** such that **one of the parent clauses contains T2 & the other contains T1** and if **T1 & T2 are unifiable**, then **neither T1 nor T2 should appear in the resolvent**. We call **T1 & T2 Complementary literals. Use the substitution produced by the unification to create the resolvent.** If there is more than one pair of complementary literals, only one pair should be omitted from the resolvent.

    3.3. If the **resolvent is an empty clause, then a contradiction has been found**. If it is not, then add it to the set of clauses available to the procedure.

4.6 Examples:

4.6.1 Example 1:

Consider the following facts.

i) The member of the St. Bridge club are Joe, Sally, Bill and Ellen.
ii) Joe is married to Sally.
iii) Bill is Ellen's brother.
iv) The spouse of every married person in the club is also in the club.
v) The last meeting of the club was at Joe's house.

1) Translate the above sentences into formulas in predicate logic.
2) Prove that last meeting of the club was at Sally's house.
3) Prove that Ellen is not married.

Formulas in predicate logic:

i)   memberOf (Joe, Club)
       memberOf (Sally, Club)
       memberOf (Bill, Club)
       memberOf (Ellen, Club)

ii)   Married (Joe, Sally)

iii)   Brother (Bill, Ellen)

iv) $\forall x, \forall y$: Married (x, y) $\wedge$ memberOf (x, Club) $\rightarrow$ memberOf (y, Club)
      $\forall x, \forall y$: Married (x, y) $\wedge$ memberOf (y, Club) $\rightarrow$ memberOf (x, Club)

v)   lastMeetingAt (Club, houseOf(Joe))

In order to prove some axioms, we need to assert some obvious axioms such as follows:

vi)   People do not get married to their brothers.
      $\forall x, \forall y$: Married (x, y) $\rightarrow$ $\neg$ Brother (x, y) $\wedge$ $\neg$ Brother (y, x)

∀x, ∀y: Brother (x, y) → ¬ Married (x, y) ∧ ¬ Married (y, x)

vii) People do not marry themselves.
∀x: ¬ Married (x, x)

viii) Marriage is a symmetric relationship.
∀x, y: Married (x, y) → Married (y, x)

ix) Spouses live in the same house.
∀x, y: Married (x, y) → equal (houseOf(x), houseOf(y))

x) Every person is married to only one other person.
∀x, y, z Married (x, y) → ¬ Married (y, z) ∧ ¬ Married (x, z)

xi) If x is a member of club, he/she is either Joe, Sally, Bill or Ellen
¬ memberOf (x, Club) V equal (x, Joe) V equal (x, Sally) V equal (x, Bill) V equal (x, Ellen)

Proof: Last meeting of the club was at Sally's house

We'll prove this directly using the given axioms:

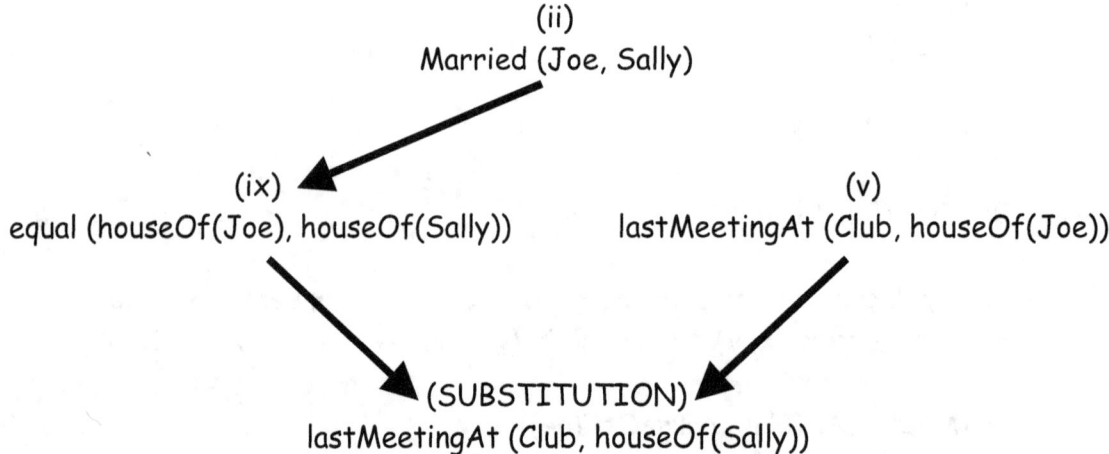

Thus, PROVED.

Proof: Ellen is not married

We'll prove this using the method of refutation (contradiction), Let's start by assuming that Ellen is Married.

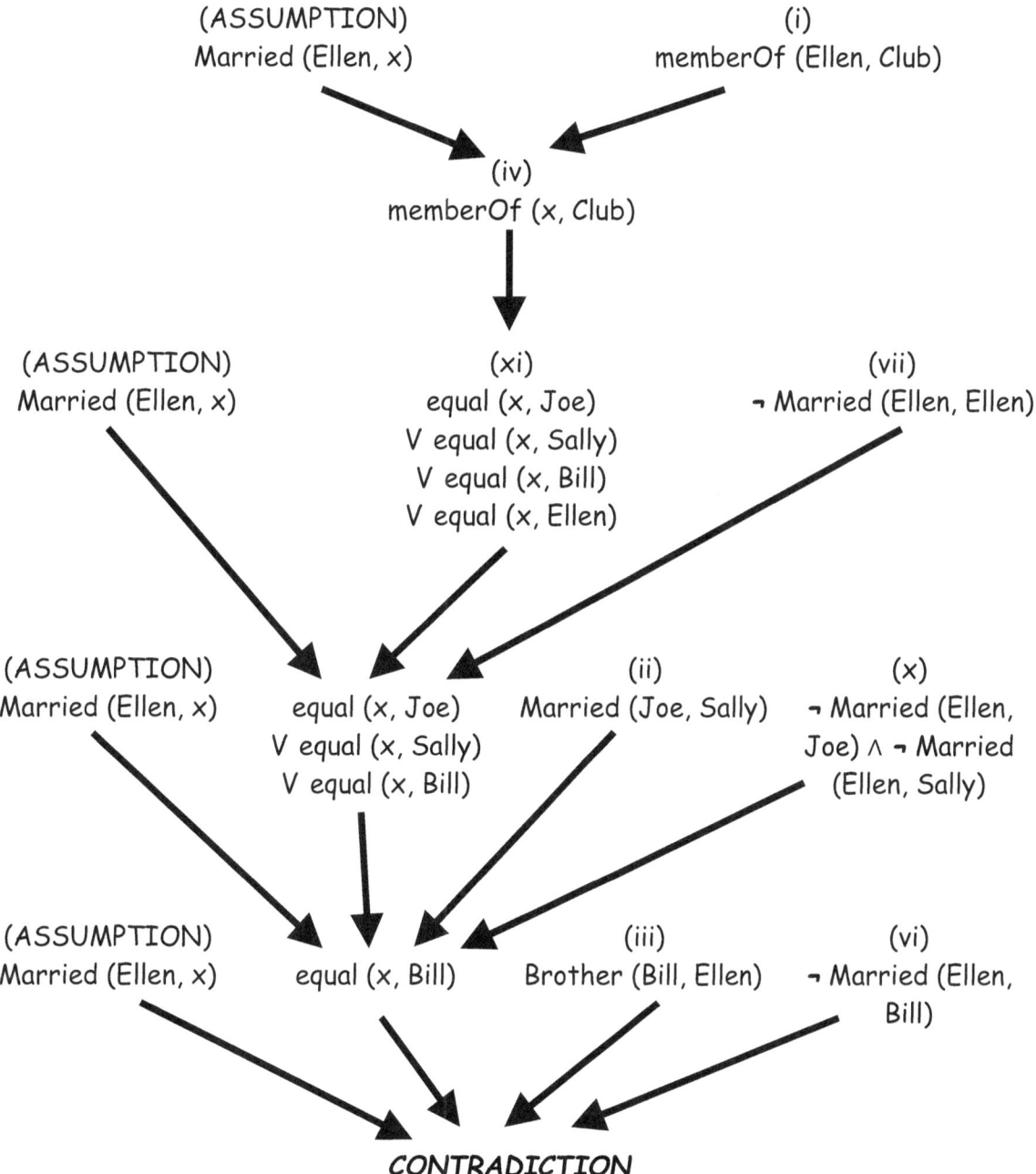

Thus, PROVED.

4.6.2 Example 2:

Consider the following axioms:

i) Anyone whom Mary loves is a football star.
ii) Any student who does not pass does not play.
iii) John is a student.
iv) Any student who does not study does not pass.
v) Anyone who does not play is not a football star.

Prove using Resolution - "If John doesn't study, Mary doesn't love John."

Formulas in predicate logic:

i) $\forall x:$ Love (Marry, x) $\rightarrow$ Football Star(x)

ii) $\forall x: \neg$ Exam (x, Pass) $\rightarrow \neg$ Play (x, Football)

iii) Student(John)

iv) $\forall x: \neg$ Study (x) $\rightarrow \neg$ Exam (x, Pass)

v) $\forall x: \neg$ Play (x, Football) $\rightarrow \neg$ Football Star(x)

In order to prove some axioms, we need to assert some obvious axioms such as follows:

vi) Any student who study, passes the exam.
$\forall x:$ Study (x) $\rightarrow$ Exam (x, Pass)

vii) Any student who pass, plays football.
$\forall x:$ Exam (x, Pass) $\rightarrow$ Play (x, Football)

viii) Anyone who plays is a football star.
$\forall x:$ Play (x, Football) $\rightarrow$ Football Star(x)

ix) Mary love anyone who is a football star.
$\forall x:$ Football Star(x) $\rightarrow$ Love (Marry, x)
$\forall x: \neg$ Football Star(x) $\rightarrow \neg$ Love (Marry, x)

Proof: If John doesn't study, Mary doesn't love John

We'll prove this using the method of refutation (contradiction), Let's start by assuming that John studies.

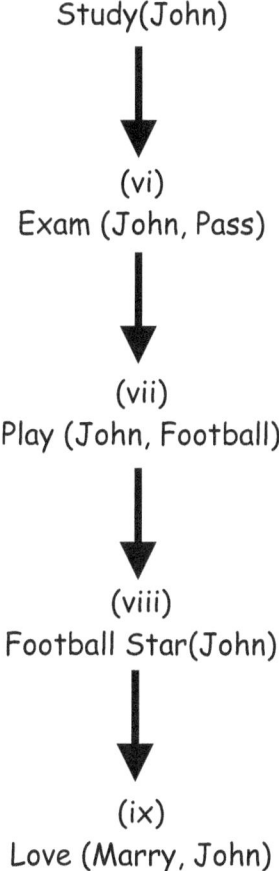

If John studies, Mary loves John. Thus, we can conclude that if John doesn't study, Mary doesn't love John.

4.6.3 Example 3:

Consider the following sentences:

i) Raj likes all kinds of food.
ii) Apples are food.
iii) Anything anyone eats and isn't killed by is food.
iv) Sachin eats peanuts and is still alive.
v) Vinod eats everything Sachin eats.

Now, attempt following:

A. Translate these sentences into formulas in predicate logic as well as clause form.
B. Use resolution to answer the question, "What food does Vinod eat?"
C. Use resolution to prove that Raj likes peanuts.

Formulas in predicate logic:

i) $\forall x: Food(x) \rightarrow Like(Raj, x)$

ii) $Food(Apples)$

iii) $\forall x, \forall y: Eats(x, y) \wedge \neg Killed(x) \rightarrow Food(y)$

iv) $Eats(Sachin, Peanuts) \wedge \neg Killed(Sachin)$

v) $\forall x: Eats(Sachin, x) \rightarrow Eats(Vinod, x)$
   $\forall x: \neg Eats(Sachin, x) \rightarrow \neg Eats(Vinod, x)$

In order to prove some axioms, we need to assert some obvious axioms such as follows:

vi) Sachin eats everything Vinod eats.

   $\forall x: Eats(Vinod, x) \rightarrow Eats(Sachin, x)$
   $\forall x: \neg Eats(Vinod, x) \rightarrow \neg Eats(Sachin, x)$

Formulas in clause form:

a) ¬ Food(x) V Like (Raj, x)

b) Food(Apples)

c) ¬ Eats (x, y) V Killed(x) V Food(x)

d) Eats (Sachin, Peanuts) ∧ ¬ Killed(Sachin)

e) Eats (Sachin, x) V ¬ Eats (Vinod, x)

f) Eats (Vinod, x) V ¬ Eats (Sachin, x)

Resolution: What food does Vinod eat?

We'll prove this using the method of refutation (contradiction), Let's start with the contradictory statement: Vinod does not eat 'x'.

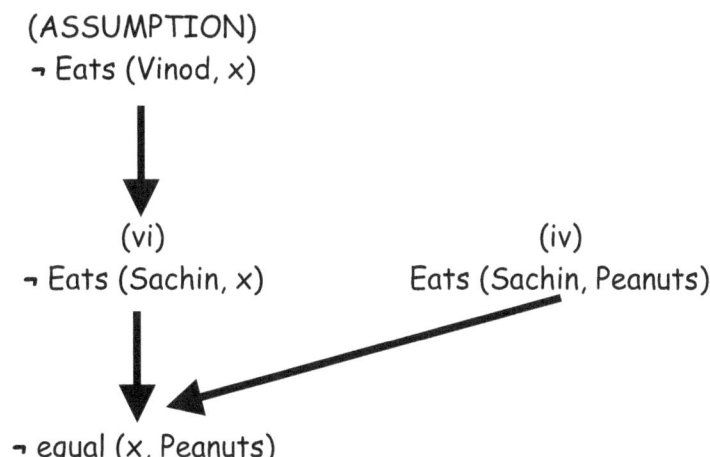

As per contradiction, Vinod doesn't eat Peanuts. Thus, we can conclude that Vinod eats Peanuts.

Proof: Raj likes Peanuts

We'll prove this using the method of refutation (contradiction), Let's start by assuming that Raj doesn't like Peanuts.

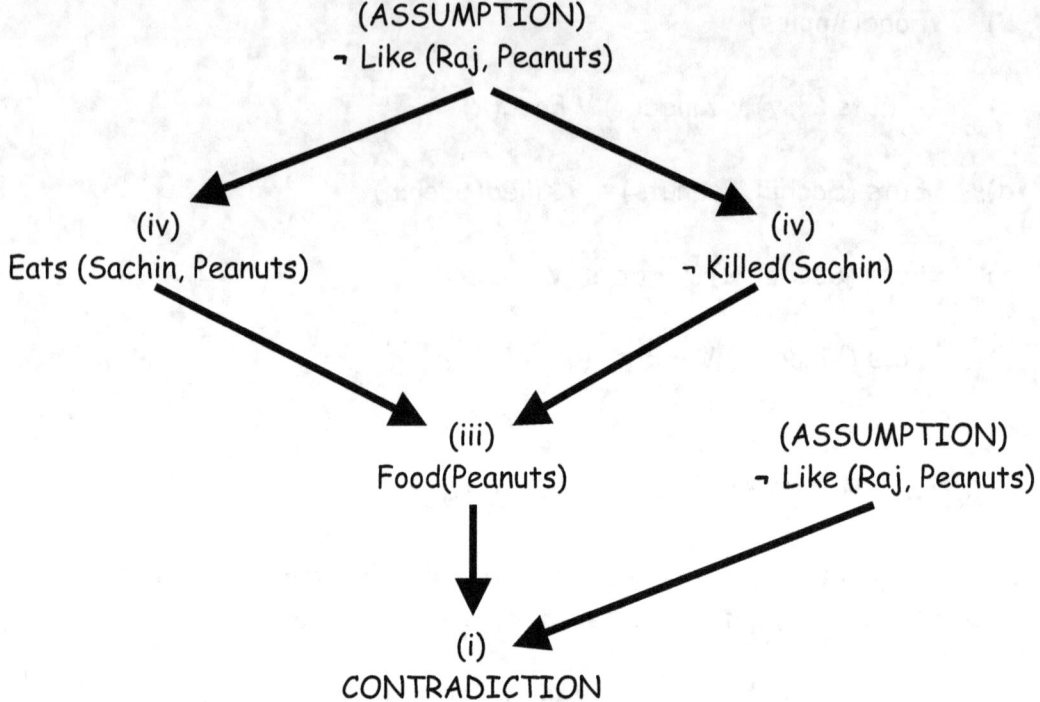

Thus, PROVED.

4.6.4 Example 4:

What is wrong with the following arguments?

i) Men are widely distributed over the earth.
ii) Socrates is a man.
iii) Therefore, Socrates is widely distributed over the earth.

How should the facts represented by these sentences be represented in logic so that this problem does not arise?

The problem is that statement (i) is universally quantified while statement (ii) pertains only to Socrates. So, we'd have to use universal elimination to be able to derive statement (iii). The problem is also in the formulation of the first statement. We might imagine a formulation like:

$\forall y, \exists x$: (PlaceOnEarth(y) ∧ Man(x) → On (y, x))

Remove existential quantifiers:
$\forall y$: (PlaceOnEarth(y) ∧ Man(f(y)) → On (y, f(y)))

The conclusion that is being made would be:
$\forall y$: (PlaceOnEarth(y) ∧ Man(Socrates) → On (y, Socrates))

Where On (y, x) means that x can be found on place y. This would express something close to what the first statement says. For any place on earth, one can find some man there (and therefore, men are widely distributed throughout the Earth).

4.6.5 Example 5:

Translate these sentences into formulas in predicate logic.

1. John likes all kinds of food.
2. Apples are food.
3. Chicken is food.
4. Anything anyone eats and isn't killed-by is food.
5. Bill eats peanuts and is still alive.
6. Sue eats everything Bill eats.

Convert the formulas into clauses. Prove that John likes peanuts using resolution.

Formulas in predicate logic:

i) $\forall x: Food(x) \rightarrow Like(John, x)$

ii) $Food(Apples)$

iii) $Food(Chicken)$

iv) $\forall x, \forall y: Eats(x, y) \land \neg Killed(x) \rightarrow Food(y)$

v) $Eats(Bill, Peanuts) \land \neg Killed(Bill)$

vi) $\forall x: Eats(Bill, x) \rightarrow Eats(Sue, x)$
$\forall x: \neg Eats(Bill, x) \rightarrow \neg Eats(Sue, x)$

In order to prove some axioms, we need to assert some obvious axioms such as follows:

vii) Bill eats everything Sue eats.

$\forall x: Eats(Sue, x) \rightarrow Eats(Bill, x)$
$\forall x: \neg Eats(Sue, x) \rightarrow \neg Eats(Bill, x)$

Formulas in clause form:

a) ¬ Food(x) V Like (John, x)

b) Food(Apples)

c) Food(Chicken)

d) ¬ Eats (x, y) V Killed(x) V Food(x)

e) Eats (Bill, Peanuts) ∧ ¬ Killed(Bill)

f) Eats (Bill, x) V ¬ Eats (Sue, x)

g) Eats (Sue, x) V ¬ Eats (Bill, x)

Proof: John likes Peanuts

We'll prove this using the method of refutation (contradiction), Let's start by assuming that John doesn't like Peanuts.

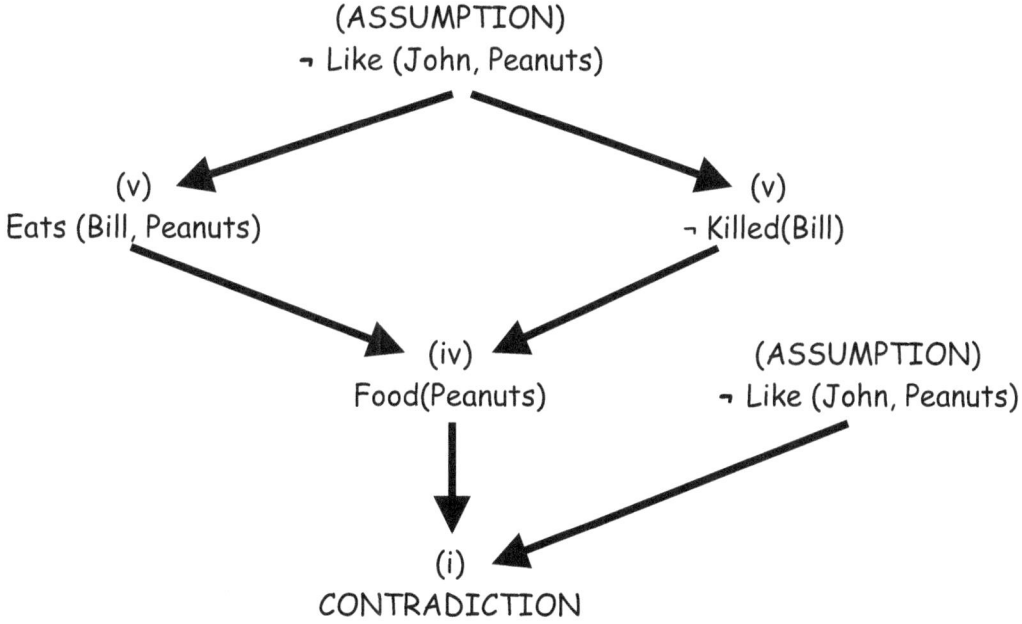

Thus, PROVED.

Chapter 5

Representing Knowledge Using Rules

5.1 Procedural versus Declarative Knowledge:

Sr. No.	Declarative Representation	Procedural Representation
1	Declarative knowledge is defined as the factual information which is stored in memory and also it is known to be static in nature.	The procedural knowledge is generally a compiled or a processed form of the information. It is related to the performance of some task.
2	Declarative knowledge involves knowing that something is the case.	Procedural knowledge involves knowing how to do something.
3	For example: B is the second letter of the English alphabet.	For example: a computer program to carry out a specific task.
4	Higher level of abstraction.	Lower level of abstraction.
5	Good modifiability & readability.	Poor modifiability & readability.
6	Poor computational efficiency.	Good computational efficiency.
7	Better for end-users.	Better for knowledge engineers.
8	It is also known as descriptive knowledge & propositional knowledge.	---

5.2 Logic Programming:

Logic programming is a programming paradigm which is largely based on *formal logic*. Any program written in a logic programming language is **a set of sentences in logical form,** expressing facts & rules about some problem domain. There are several logic programming systems in use, **PROLOG** is one of them. In all of the *logic programming languages, rules are written in the form of clauses* as follows:

H :- B1, …, Bn.

and are **read declaratively as logical implications**:

H if B1 and … and Bn.

H is called the **head of the rule** & $B_1, …, B_n$ is called the **body of the rule**. Facts are **rules that have no body**, and are written in the **simplified form** as follows: H.

Consider the following *example*:

A. Logical representation

$\forall x: pet(x) \land small(x) \rightarrow apartmentpet(x)$
$\forall x: cat(x) \land dog(x) \rightarrow pet(x)$
$\forall x: poodle(x) \rightarrow dog(x) \land small(x)$
poodle (fluffy)

B. Prolog representation

apartmentpet (x) :- pet(x), small (x)
pet (x) :- cat (x)
pet (x) :- dog(x)
dog(x) :- poodle (x)
small (x) :- poodle(x)
poodle (fluffy)

A PROLOG program consists of several logical assertions where each one is a **horn clause (a clause in its atomic form).**

5.3 Forward versus Backward Reasoning:

The objective of a search procedure is to find a **path between initial state & goal state**. There are **two directions** in which the search procedure could proceed:

> **Forward Search**, that **starts from the initial state**. It is a **data-driven** technique of deriving a solution from a set of rules. This is known as a data-driven search because it **starts from a set of data & ends up at the goal**. In forward reasoning, the **left-hand sides of the rules are matched** against the current state & **right-hand sides are used to generate the new state**.

> **Backward Search**, that **starts from the goal state**. It is a **goal-driven** technique of deriving a solution from a set of rules. This is known as a goal-driven search because it **starts by examining the goal** that we're trying to prove, then the search figures out the **actions that can lead to the goal state**. In backward reasoning, the **right-hand sides of the rules are matched** against the current state & **left-hand sides are used to generate the new state**.

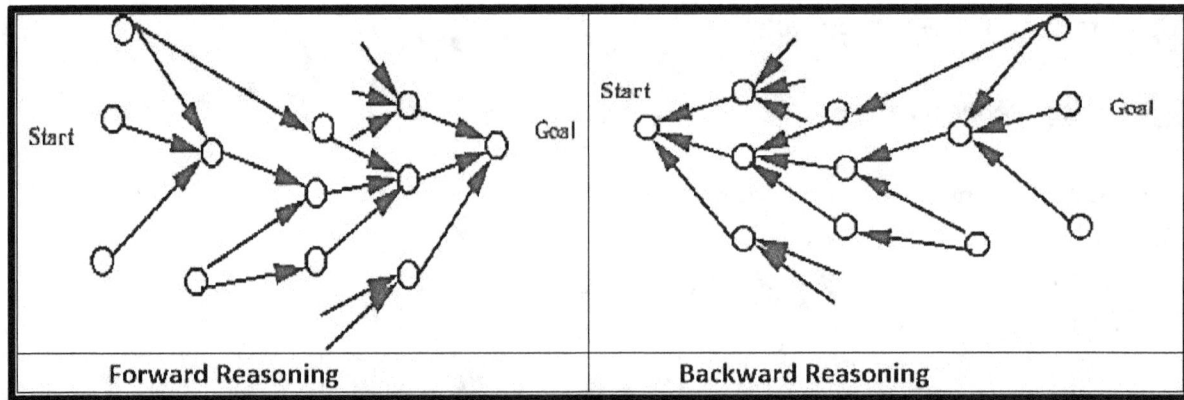

Figure 5.1: Forward versus Backward Reasoning

Consider an **example** of solving **8 puzzle problem**. The **rules** are defined as follows:

Square 1 empty & square 2 contains tile n →
Square 2 empty & square 1 contains the tile n

Square 1 empty & square 4 contains tile n →
Square 4 empty & square 1 contains the tile n

Square 2 empty & square 1 contains tile n →
Square 1 empty & square 2 contains the tile n

- ➤ ***Reason forward from initial state***: Begin building a tree by starting with the ***initial state configuration at the root of the tree***. Generate the next level of tree by finding all rules whose ***left-hand side matches against the root node***. The ***right-hand side is used to create new configurations***. Generate the next level by considering the nodes in the previous level and applying to it all the rules whose ***left-hand side match***.

- ➤ ***Reason backward from the goal state***: Begin building a tree starting with the ***goal state configuration at the root of the tree***. Generate the next level of tree by finding all rules whose ***right-hand side matches against the root node***. The ***left-hand side is used to create new configurations***. Generate the next level by considering the nodes in the previous level and applying to it all rules whose ***right-hand side match***.

In the case of the 8-puzzle, it does not make much difference whether we reason forward or backward; about the same number of paths will be explored in either case. But this is not always true. **Four factors** influence the question of whether it is **better to reason forward or backward**:

1. **Are there more possible start states or goal states?** We would like to move from the smaller set of states to the larger (hence, easier to find) set of states.

2. **In which direction is the branching factor (i.e., the average number of nodes that can be reached directly from a single node) greater?** We would like to proceed in the direction with the lower branching factor.

3. **Will the program be asked to justify its reasoning process to a user?** If so, it is important to proceed in the direction that corresponds more closely with the user's way of thinking.

4. **What kind of event is going to trigger a problem-solving process?** If it is the arrival of a new fact, forward reasoning makes sense. If it is a query to which a response is desired, backward reasoning is more natural.

Instead of searching either forward or backward, you can search both simultaneously. That is, start forward from an initial state & backward from a goal state simultaneously until the paths meets. This strategy is called ***Bi-Directional Search***.

5.4 PROLOG uses Backward Chaining:

PROLOG is a logic programming language that uses **backward chaining** to solve a problem because it is **more efficient than forward chaining** when there are **large collections of axioms**.

A **PROLOG program** consists of a collection of **Horn (atomic) clauses**. Each clause consists of a **head predicate** & **body predicates**:

H :- B$_1$, B$_2$, ..., B$_n$.

> A clause is either a rule,
> e.g. **snowy(X) :- rainy(X), cold(X).**
> meaning: "If X is rainy and X is cold then this implies that X is snowy"

> Or a clause is a fact,
> e.g. **rainy(Rochester).**
> meaning "Rochester is rainy."

> This fact is identical to the rule with **true** as the body predicate:
> **rainy(Rochester) :- true**

Consider the following **example**:

A. Logical representation

$\forall x$: pet(x) $\wedge$ small (x) $\rightarrow$ apartmentpet(x)
$\forall x$: cat(x) $\wedge$ dog(x) $\rightarrow$ pet(x)
$\forall x$: poodle (x) $\rightarrow$ dog (x) $\wedge$ small (x)
poodle (fluffy)

B. Prolog representation

apartmentpet (x) :- pet(x), small (x)
pet (x) :- cat (x)
pet (x) :- dog(x)
dog(x) :- poodle (x)
small (x) :- poodle(x)
poodle (fluffy) :- true

In the above example, we can see that the **PROLOG representation** of the axioms starts with the **goal of the axiom in the head part** of the clause & the **preconditions to satisfy the goal are written in the body part** of the clause. Thus, **we can say that PROLOG uses Backward Chaining** methodology to solve a particular problem.

5.5 Conflict Resolution in Rule-Based System:

Conflict resolution strategies are used in production systems such as in **rule-based expert systems**, to **help in choosing which production rule to apply**. The need for such a strategy arises when the **conditions of two or more rules are satisfied** by the currently known facts.

Conflict resolution strategies fall into **several categories** such as:

1. **Specificity**: If all of the conditions of two or more rules are satisfied, choose the **rule according to how specific its conditions are**.

2. **Recency**: When two or more rules could be chosen, favor **the one that matches the most recently added facts**, as these are most likely to describe the current situation.

3. **Not Previously Used**: If all of the conditions of two or more rules are satisfied, choose the **rule that has not been used previously by the same facts**. This helps to prevent the system from entering infinite loops.

4. **Order**: Pick the **first applicable rule in order of presentation**. This is the strategy that Prolog interpreters use by default,

5. **Arbitrary Choice**: **Pick a rule at random**. This has the merit of being simple to compute.

Types of **Conflict resolution strategies** are as follows:

1. Based on Order of the Rules:

The simplest way is to resolve the conflict is to **consider the particular order in which the rules have been specified**, such as the physical order in which they are presented to the system. Then priority is given to the rules in the order in which they appear.

We can use **First-in First-serve** methodology that will **apply the very first rule** that matches the given facts.

We can also use **Last-in First-serve** methodology that will **apply the last rule** that matches the given facts.

2. Based on Prioritization of the Rules:

Another way that conflict can be resolved is by **prioritizing the rules** based on the importance of the rule. User's tend to trust this kind of reasoning more than the one which relies on ordering of rules.

3. Based on the State Generated by the Applied Rules:

Suppose that there are **several rules waiting to be applied**. One way of selecting a rule among them is to **apply all of them temporarily** & to examine the results of each one. Then, using a **heuristic function that can evaluate each of the resulting states**, **compare the merits** of the results, & **select the most preferred one**. Throw away the remaining ones.

Chapter 6

Symbolic Reasoning Under Uncertainty

6.1 Introduction to Reasoning:

Reasoning is the act of deriving a conclusion from certain known facts using a given methodology. When a system is required to do something, that it has not been explicitly told how to do, it must reason. It must figure out what it needs to do from what it already knows.

For **example**, if we know: **Robins are birds & all birds have wings**. Then if we ask: **Do robins have wings?** Some reasoning has to be done to answer the question.

Reasoning is drawing inference from known facts. Many types of Reasoning have been identified & recognized. There are **three different approaches to reasoning**:

1. **Symbolic reasoning**
2. **Statistical reasoning**
3. **Fuzzy logic reasoning**

Our concern in this chapter is to study **Symbolic Reasoning**. It involves manipulating symbols & expressions according to mathematical & logical rules,

---

Fun Fact:

The **IQ (Intelligence quotient)** is the summation of **mathematical reasoning & logical reasoning** capabilities of a person.

The **EQ (Emotional Quotient)** depends mostly on **non-logical reasoning** capabilities of a person.

6.2 Introduction to Non-Monotonic Reasoning:

A logic is said to be monotonic if anything that could be concluded before a clause is added can still be concluded after it is added; adding knowledge does not reduce the set of propositions that can be derived.

A logic is said to be non-monotonic if some conclusions can be invalidated (discarded) by adding more knowledge.

Non-monotonic reasoning is based on supplementing the truth with beliefs or assumptions that are made due to the lack of evidence. For an instance, a state S will be assumed to be true as long as there is no evidence to the contrary.

A *non-monotonic reasoning* system tracks a set of tentative beliefs & revises those beliefs when the knowledge is derived.

This is *similar to the human being's way of reasoning* & thus, *non-monotonic reasoning* is of significant importance in Artificial Intelligence.

Non-monotonic systems are harder to deal with than monotonic systems. This is due to the fact that when a statement is deleted because it's *"no more valid"*, other related statements have to be backtracked & they should either be deleted or new proofs have to be found for them. This is called *dependency directed backtracking (DDB)*.

In order to *implement non-monotonic reasoning*, following *key issues* must be addressed:

1. How can *knowledge base be extended* to allow inferences to be made on the basis of lack of knowledge as well as on the presence of it?

2. How can the *knowledge base be updated* properly when a new fact is added to the system or when an old one is removed?

3. How can *knowledge be used to help resolve conflicts* when there are several inconsistent non-monotonic inferences that could be drawn?

6.3 Logics for Non-Monotonic Reasoning:

6.3.1 Default Reasoning:

Non-monotonic reasoning is based on **default reasoning** or "**most probabilistic choice**". It draws conclusion based on what is most likely to be true. A **computational description** of **default reasoning** must relate the **lack of information on X to conclude on Y**. **Default reasoning** is defined as follows:

Definition 1: If X is not known, then conclude Y.
Definition 2: If X can't be proved, then conclude Y.
Definition 3: If X can't be proved in some allocated amount of time then conclude Y.

There are **two approaches** to carry out **default reasoning**: **Non-monotonic Logic** & **Default Logic**.

6.3.1.1 Non-monotonic Logic:

Non-monotonic logic system provides a **basis for default reasoning** in which a system of the language of **first-order predicate logic** is augmented with a **modal operator M**, which can be read as "is consistent with everything we know". For example, consider the following formula:

$$\forall x, y: Related(x, y) \land M\, GetAlong(x, y) \rightarrow WillDefend(x, y)$$

The above formulae can be read as: "For all x & y, if x & y are related and if the fact that x gets along with y is consistent with everything we know, then conclude that x will defend y".

6.3.1.2 Default Logic:

Default logic is an alternative for performing **default reasoning**. It introduces a **new class of inference rules**. The **inference rules** are of the **following form**:

$$\frac{A : B}{C}$$

The above rule is read as: "If A is provable & it is consistent to assume B then conclude C ". Here, A is known as the prerequisite, B as the justification, and C as the consequent.

For example, rule that **"birds typically fly"** would be represented as:

$$\frac{Bird\ (x) : Flies\ (x)}{Flies\ (x)}$$

The above rule says: "If x is a bird & the claim that x flies is consistent with what we know, then we can infer that x flies".

6.3.2 Methods of Logical Reasoning:

Generally, there are **three kinds of logical reasoning**: Deduction, Induction & Abduction.

6.3.2.1 Deduction:

Reasoning other facts from known facts & general principles. Guarantees that the conclusion is true.

Modus Ponens: a valid form of argument affirming the antecedent.

If it is rainy, John carries an umbrella

$$\frac{It\ is\ rainy}{John\ carries\ an\ umbrella}$$

--------------------The line resembles "therefore" --------------------

If p then q

$$\frac{p}{q}$$

Modus Tollens: a valid form of argument denying the consequent.

If it is rainy, John carries an umbrella

$$\frac{John\ does\ not\ carry\ an\ umbrella}{It\ is\ not\ rainy}$$

-------------------The line resembles "because" -------------------

$$\text{If p then q}$$
$$\frac{not\ q}{not\ p}$$

6.3.2.2 Induction:

Reasoning from many past instances to all future instances.

- ### Good Movie

    Fact: You have liked all movies starring Mary.
    Inference: You will like her next movie.

- ### Birds

    Facts: Woodpeckers, swifts, eagles, finches have four toes on each foot.
    Inductive Inference: All birds have 4 toes on each foot. (Note: Partridges have only 3)

- ### Objects

    Facts: Cars, bottles, blocks fall if not held up.
    Inductive Inference: If not supported, an object will fall. (Note: an unsupported helium balloon will rise.)

- ### Medicine

    Noted: People who had cowpox did not get smallpox.
    Induction: Cowpox prevents smallpox.
Problem: Sometime inference is correct, sometimes not correct.

Advantage: Inductive inference may be useful even if not correct. It generates a proposition which may be validated deductively.

6.3.2.3 Abduction:

Common form of human reasoning. In Abductive reasoning, you make an assumption which, if true, together with your general knowledge, will explain the facts.

- *Dating*

    Fact: Mary asks John to a party.
    Abductive Inferences: Mary likes John.
    John is Mary's last choice.
    Mary wants to make someone else jealous.

- *Smoking House*

    Fact: A large amount of black smoke is coming from a home.
    Abduction1: The house is on fire.
    Abduction2: Bad cook.

- *Diagnosis*

    Facts: A thirteen-year-old boy has a sharp pain in his right side, a fever, and a high white blood count.
    Abductive Inference: Appendicitis.

Problem: Not always correct; many explanations possible.
Advantage: Understandable conclusions.

Statistical Reasoning

7.1 Introduction to Statistical Reasoning:

We have described several representation techniques that can be used to model problems in which a particular fact is believed to be true, believed to be false or not considered at all. But for some kind of problems, it is useful to be able to **describe beliefs that are not certain but for which there is some supporting evidence**. There are **two such kind of problems**:

1. **Problems that contain genuine randomness**. For example, Card Games.

2. **Problems that behaves normally unless there is an exception**. The difficulty in these kind of problems is that there are many possible exceptions than we need to enumerate explicitly. Tasks such as medical diagnosis falls in to this category.

For such problems, **statistical measures** may serve a very useful function to **derive the summaries of the problem environment**. Rather than looking for all possible exceptions, we can use a **numerical summary** that tells us **how often an exception of some sort can be expected to occur**.

Our concern in this chapter is to study **schemes for treating uncertainty in rule based systems**. The most commonly used schemes that we'll study are:

- Adding certainty factors.

- Adoptions of Dempster-Shafer belief functions.

- Inclusion of fuzzy logic.

7.2 Probability & Bays' Theorem:

An *important goal* for a *problem-solving system* is to *collect evidence* as the system goes along & to *modify its behavior* on the basis of the *evidence*. To model this behavior, we need a *statistical theory of evidence*. *Bayesian statistics* is such a theory. The *fundamental notion of Bayesian statistics* is that of *conditional probability: P (H | E)*

The above expression can be read as **the probability of Hypothesis H given that we have observed evidence E**. To compute this, we need to take into account **the prior probability of H** (the probability that we would assign to H if we had no evidence) & **the extent to which E provides evidence of H**.

To do this we need to define a universe that contains an exhaustive, mutually exclusive set of H_i's, among which we are trying to discriminate. Following is what **Bayes' theorem** states:

$$P(H_i \mid E) = \frac{P(E \mid H_i) \cdot P(H_i)}{\sum_{n=1}^{k} P(E \mid H_n) \cdot P(H_n)}$$

Where,

P (Hi | E) = The probability that hypothesis Hi is true given evidence E.

P (E | Hi) = The probability that we will observe evidence E given that hypothesis Hi is true.

P(Hi) = The probability that hypothesis Hi is true in the absence of any specific evidence. These probabilities are called prior probabilities.

K = The number of possible hypothesis.

Suppose, for example, that we want to examine the geological evidence at a particular location to determine whether that would be a good place to dig for finding a desired mineral.
If we know the prior probabilities of finding each of the various minerals and we know the probabilities that if a mineral is present then certain physical characteristics will

be observed, then we can use Bayes' formula to compute how likely it is that the various minerals are present.

7.3 Certainty Factors & Rule-Based Systems:

Certainty factor is a practical way of **compromising on a pure Bayesian system**. The basic idea is to **add certainty factors to rules**, & **use these to calculate the measure of belief in some hypothesis**. We will use MYCIN as an example here which uses LISP. MYCIN is an Expert System which attempts to recommend appropriate therapies for patients with bacterial infections.

MYCIN uses the rules to **reason Backwards** from its **goal of finding significant disease-causing organisms** to the **clinical data available**.

MYCIN represents most of its **diagnostic knowledge as a set of rules**. Each rule has associated with it a **certainty factor**, which is a measure of **the extent to which the evidence** (given in the rule's antecedent) **supports the conclusion** (given in the rule's consequent).

Based on the **certainty factor**, MYCIN identities of the disease-causing organism & then attempts to select a therapy by which the disease can be treated.

A **certainty factor (CF [h, e])** is defined in terms of two components:

1. **MB [h, e]** - A measure (between 0 and 1) of belief in hypothesis "h" given the evidence "e". MB measures the extent to which the evidence supports the **hypothesis**. It is **zero if the evidence fails to support the hypothesis**.

2. **MD [h, e]** - A measure (between 0 and 1) of disbelief in hypothesis "h" given the evidence "e". MD measures the extent to which the evidence supports the **negation of the hypothesis**. It is **zero if the evidence support the hypothesis**.

> Certainty Factor,
> CF [h, e] = MB [h, e] - MD [h, e]

We might have a rule as follows:

```
IF       has-spots(X)
AND      has-fever(X)
THEN     has-measles(X)    CF 0.5
```

Sometimes, **CFs need to be combined** to reflect the operation on **multiple pieces of evidence**.

Considering the above stated rule, suppose that we have already concluded **has-spots(Fred) with certainty 0.3**, & **has-fever(fred) with certainty 0.8**. To work out the **probability of has-measles(X)** we need to take account both of the **certainties of the evidence** & **the certainty factor attached to the rule**. The **certainty associated with the conjoined premise** (has-spots(Fred) AND has-fever(Fred)) is taken to be the **minimum of the certainties attached to each** (i.e. **min (0.3, 0.8) = 0.3**). The **certainty of the conclusion** is the **total certainty of the premises multiplied by the certainty factor of the rule** (i.e., **0.3 x 0.5 = 0.15**).

7.4 Bayesian Networks:

Bayesian Network is an *alternative to Certainty Factor* for *reducing the complexity of Bayesian Reasoning.*

Bayesian Network relies on the *modularity of the world* that we're trying to model. The idea is to *describe the real world*, it is *not necessary to use a huge joint probability table* to list the probabilities of all combinations. Since *most events are independent of each other*, there is *no need to consider the interactions between them*. Instead, we will use a more local representation in which we will describe clusters of events that interacts with each other. Consider the following example of *Bayesian Network*:

S: *sprinkler was on last night*
W: *grass is wet*
R: *it rained last night*

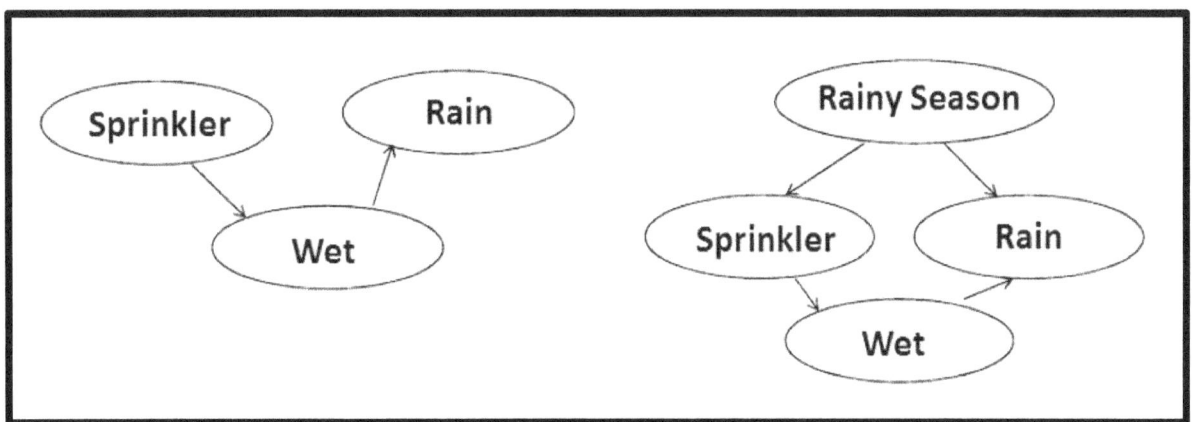

Figure 7.1: Bayesian Network

There are two different ways that propositions can influence the likelihood of each other:

1. *The first is that outcomes influence the likelihood of their symptoms.*
2. *The second is that observing a symptom influence the likelihood of all its possible outcomes.*

The *main idea behind the Bayesian network structure* is to make a clear distinction between these two kinds of influences.

The Graph in above figure is known as **DAG (Directed Acyclic Graph)** that **represents relationships among the propositions that it contains**. However, we need more information. In particular, **for each value of a parent node, we need to know what evidence is provided about the values that the child node can take**. We create a **probability table** for that. Following is an example of priority table:

Attribute	Probability
P (Wet | Sprinkler, Rain)	0.95
P (Wet | Sprinkler, ¬ Rain)	0.9
P (Wet | ¬ Sprinkler, Rain)	0.8
P (Wet | ¬ Sprinkler, ¬ Rain)	0.1
P (Sprinkler | Rainy Season)	0.0
P (Sprinkler | ¬ Rainy Season)	1.0
P (Rain | Rainy Season)	0.9
P (Rain | ¬ Rainy Season)	0.1
P (Rainy Season)	0.5

Figure 7.2: Priority Table for Bayesian Network

From the above probability table, we can infer that the prior probability of the rainy season is 0.5. Then, if it is the rainy season, the probability of rain on a given night is 0.9, if it is not, the probability is only 0.1.

When the most genuine reasoning does not seem true then we need to use an **undirected graph** in which the **arcs can be used to transmit probabilities in either direction**, depending upon where the evidence came from. But we have to **ensure that no cycle exists between the evidences**.

7.5 Dempster-Shafer Theory:

So far, we have described several techniques, all of which consider individual propositions & assigns an estimate of the degree of belief (given the evidence) to each of them. In this section, we consider an alternative technique, called **Dempster-Shafer theory**.

In **Dempster-Shafer Theory** we consider **sets of propositions** & **assign an interval** to each one of them in which the **degree of belief** must lie. The interval is of the following form:

[Belief, Plausibility]

Belief (Bel) measures the strength of the evidence in favor of a set of propositions. It ranges from 0 (indicating no evidence) to 1 (denoting certainty).

Plausibility (Pl) also ranges from 0 to 1 & it measures the extent to which evidence in the favor of ¬s leaves room for belief in s. Technically, the term plausibility refers to the acceptability measure of the propositions. It is defined as follows:

$$Pl(s) = 1 - Bel(\neg s)$$

Briefly, if we have certain evidence in favor of (¬s), then Bel(¬s) will be 1 and Pl(s) will be 0. This tells us that the only possible value for Bel(s) is also 0.

The interval, also tells about the **amount of information that we have**. If we have no evidence we say that the hypothesis is in the range of [0, 1]. As we gain more evidence, this interval can be expected to shrink & give confident answers.

Let's consider the following **example**:

Set of propositions, θ = {Allergy, Flu, Cold, Pneumonia}

We want to **attach some measure of belief to elements of θ**. But all evidences are not directly supportive of individual elements. The **key function** we use here is a **Probability Density Function, denoted by m**. The function m, is not only defined for elements of θ but also all subsets of it. The quantity **m(p) measures the amount of belief that is currently assigned to the set "p"** (subset of original set of propositions).

If **θ contains n elements** then there are **2ⁿ subsets of θ**. We must assign m so that the **sum of all the m values assigned to subsets of θ is 1**.

At the beginning, we have **m as under θ = (1.0)**.

If we get an **evidence of 0.6 magnitude** that the correct diagnosis is in the set **{Flu, Cold, Pneumonia}** then, {Flu, Cold, Pneumonia} = (0.6) & θ = (0.4).

Sometimes, we might need more information, it can be calculated as shown in the following table:

	{A, F, C} = (0.8)	θ = (0.2)
{F, C, P} = (0.6)	{F, C} = (0.48)	{F, C, P} = (0.12)
θ = (0.4)	{A, F, C} = (0.32)	θ = (0.8)

Where,
A = Allergy
F = Flu
C = Cold
P = Pneumonia

7.6 Fuzzy Logic:

In the techniques discussed so far, we haven't modified the mathematical fundamentals provided by set theory and logic. We have instead augmented those ideas with probability theory.

Fuzzy logic takes a different approach to computing **based on "degrees of truth"** rather than the usual **"true or false" (1 or 0)**.

The **motivation for fuzzy logic** is provided by the **need to represent propositions such as**:

- *John is very tall.*
- *Mary is slightly ill.*
- *Sue and Linda are close friends.*
- *Most Frenchmen are not very tall.*

Fuzzy logic includes 0 & 1 as extreme cases of truth but **also includes the various states of truth in between 0 & 1**. For example, the result of a height based comparison between two things could be "tall" or "short" but it could also be "0.3 units of tallness".

Fuzzy logic is a method of reasoning that resembles human reasoning. The approach of fuzzy logic imitates the way of decision making in humans that involves all intermediate possibilities between binary values 0 & 1.

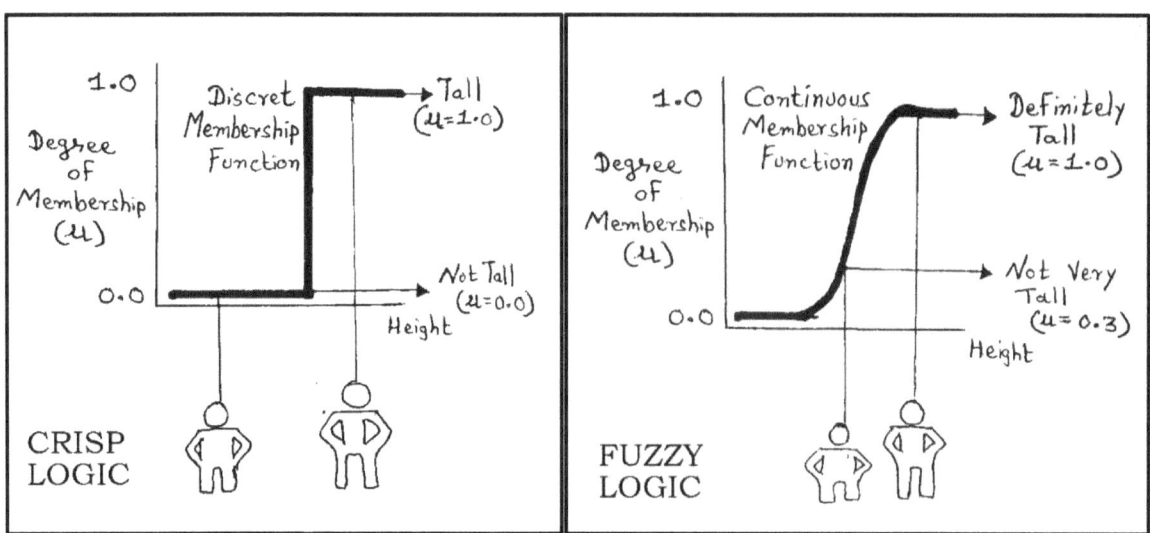

Figure 7.3: Conventional (Crisp) versus Fuzzy Logic

While traditional set theory defines set membership as a Boolean predicate, fuzzy set theory allows us to represent set membership as a function of continuous values, such as the ones shown in the above figure.

In the standard Boolean definition for tall, people are either tall or not & there must be a specific height that defines the boundary. But in case of fuzzy logic, a person's tallness increases with his/her height until the value of 1 is reached. In fuzzy logic, we can also obtain the value for measure of height that is between 0 & 1.

Once set membership has been redefined in this way, it is possible to define a reasoning system based on Fuzzy Logic.

Slot-and-Filler Structures

8.1 Semantic Nets:

Semantic net (or semantic network) is an alternative to predicate logic as a **form of knowledge representation**. It is a **two-dimensional representation** of knowledge. The idea is that we can **store our knowledge in the form of a directed graph**, with **nodes representing objects** in the world, & **arcs representing relationships** between those objects.

Let's consider the **example** given in the following figure:

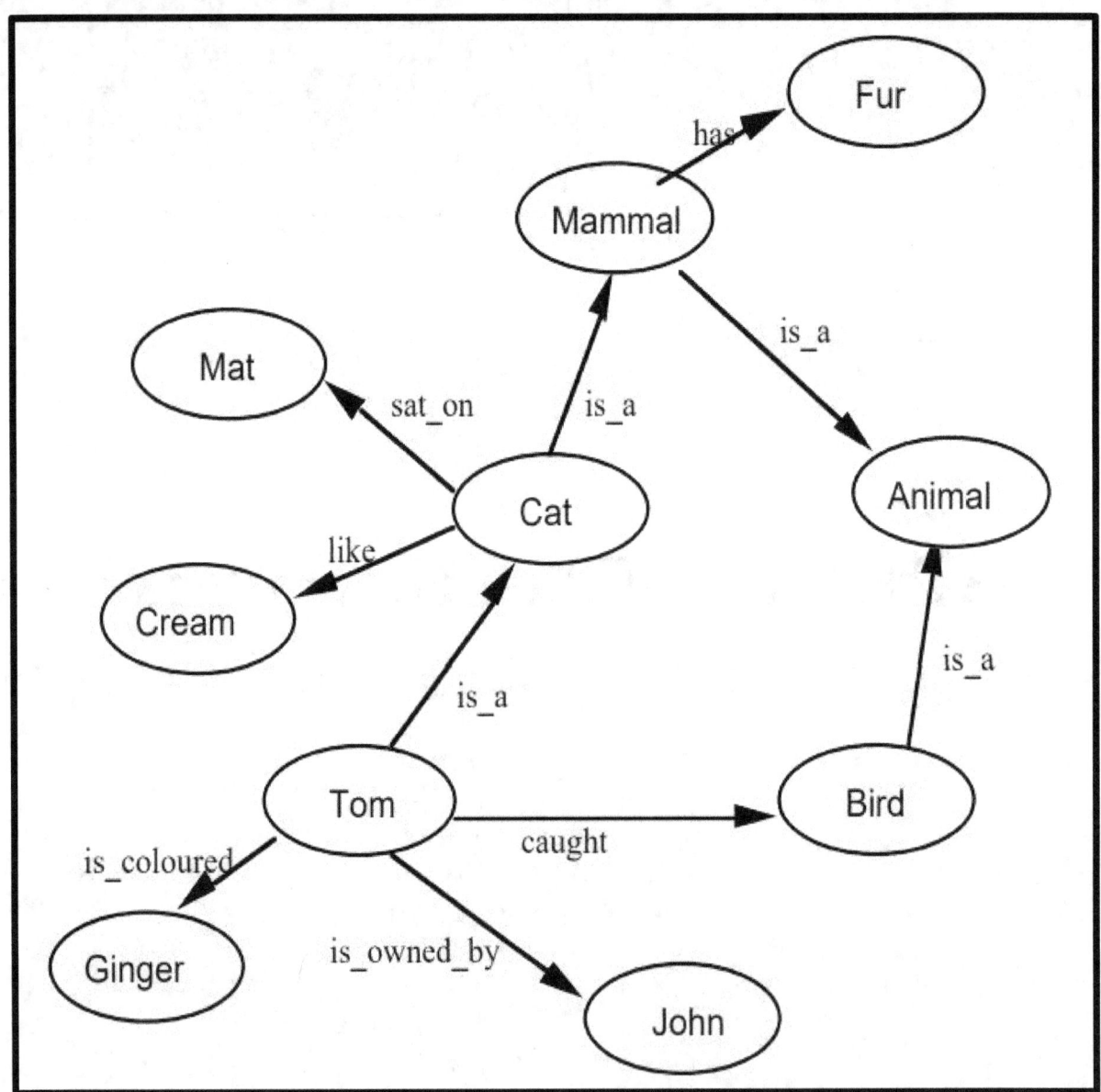

Figure 8.1: Semantic Network (Example)

The semantic net shown in the above figure is intended to represent the following propositions:

- *Tom is a cat.*
- *Tom caught a bird.*
- *Tom is owned by John.*
- *Tom is ginger in color.*
- *Cats like cream.*
- *The cat sat on the mat.*
- *A cat is a mammal.*
- *A bird is an animal.*
- *All mammals are animals.*
- *Mammals have fur.*

It is argued that rather than predicate logic, this form of representation (Semantic Networks) is **closer to the way in which human beings structure the knowledge** by building mental links between things.

Disadvantage of Semantic Nets:

The links between the objects can **only represent binary relations**. For instance, the sentence Run (Chennai-Express, Chennai, Bangalore, Today) cannot be represented directly.

Advantages of Semantic Nets:

They're **simple & easy** to understand.

They can **easily be translated in to PROLOG**.

They **convey meaning in a transparent manner**.

They have the ability to **represent default values for categories**. For an instance, if it is mentioned that **birds have wings & xyz is a bird**, it is **inferred by default** that **xyz has wings** unless it is **explicitly specified** that **xyz is a bird with no wings**.

8.1.1 Partitioned Semantic Nets:

If we want to **represent simple quantified expressions** in semantic nets then it can be done with the help of **partitioning the semantic net into a hierarchical set of spaces**, each of which corresponds to the **scope of one or more variable**.

Suppose we want to make a specific statement about a **dog named Danny who has bitten a postman named Peter**:

"**Danny the dog bit Peter the postman**"

Partitioned semantic net would easily represent this statement as an ordinary semantic network as follows:

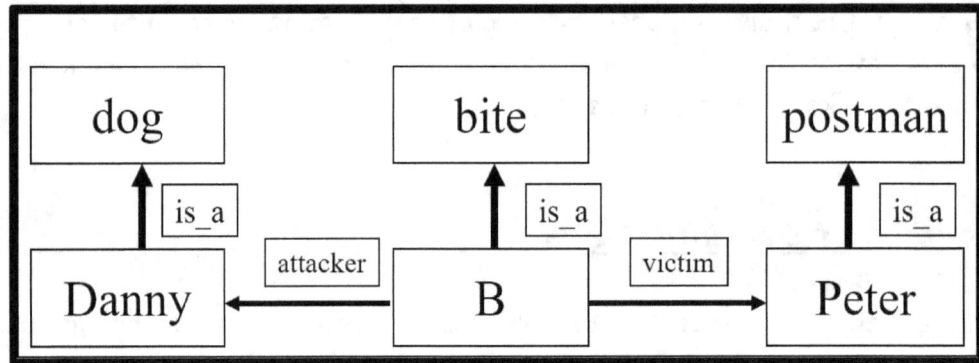

Figure 8.2: Partitioned Semantic Network (Example 1)

Consider another statement: "**Every dog has bitten a postman**". This can be represented using a universal quantifier as follows:

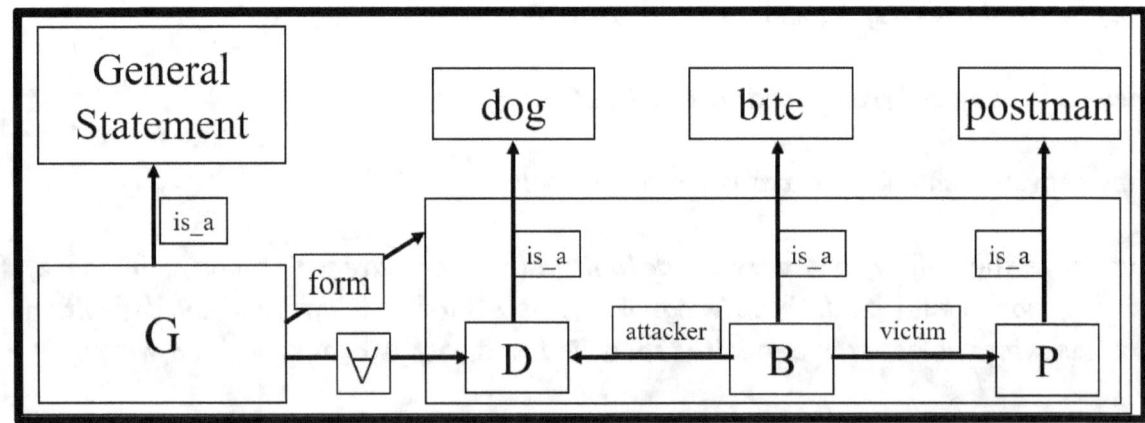

Figure 8.3: Partitioned Semantic Network (Example 2)

Consider another statement: *"Every dog has bitten every postman"*. This can be represented as follows:

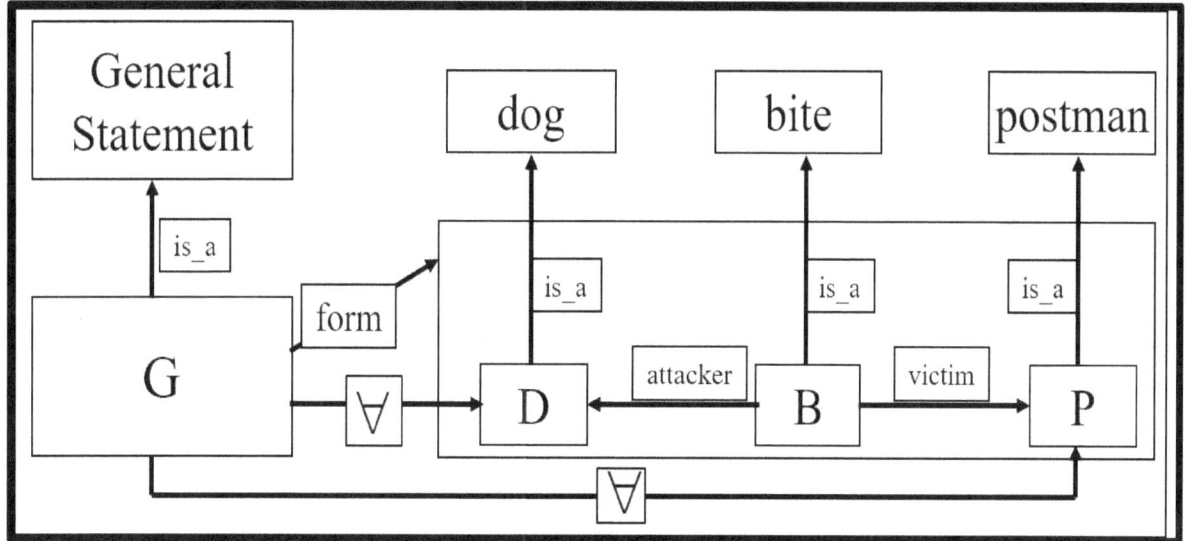

Figure 8.4: Partitioned Semantic Network (Example 3)

Consider another statement: *"Every dog in town has bitten a postman"*. This can be represented as follows:

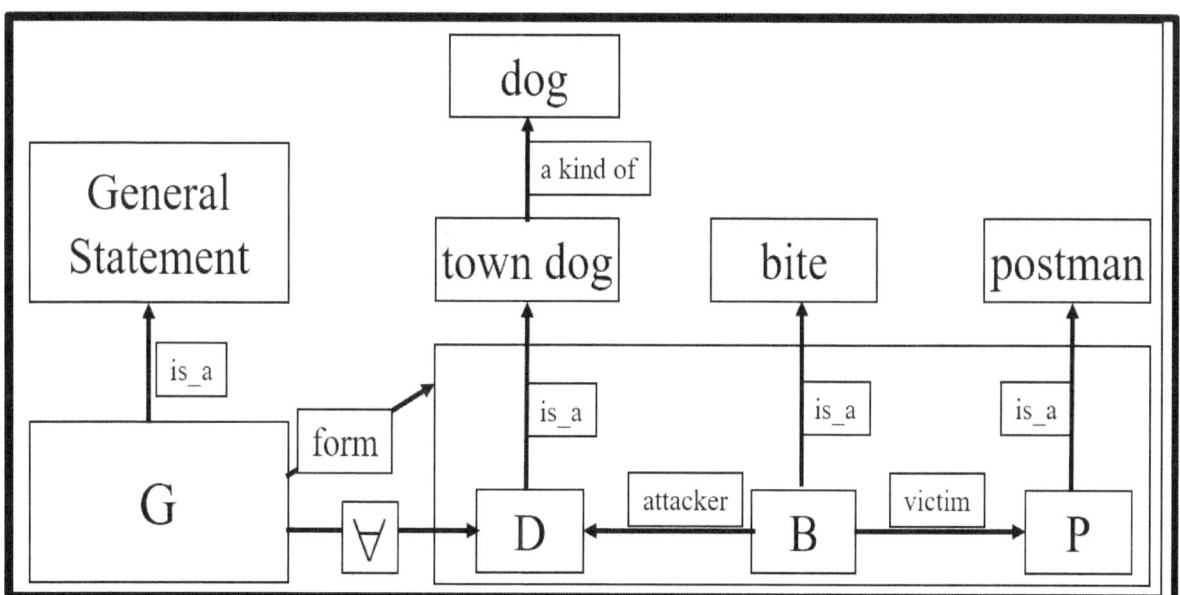

Figure 8.5: Partitioned Semantic Network (Example 4)

Consider another example: *"Sita gave the pearl garland to Hanuman"*. This can be represented as follows:

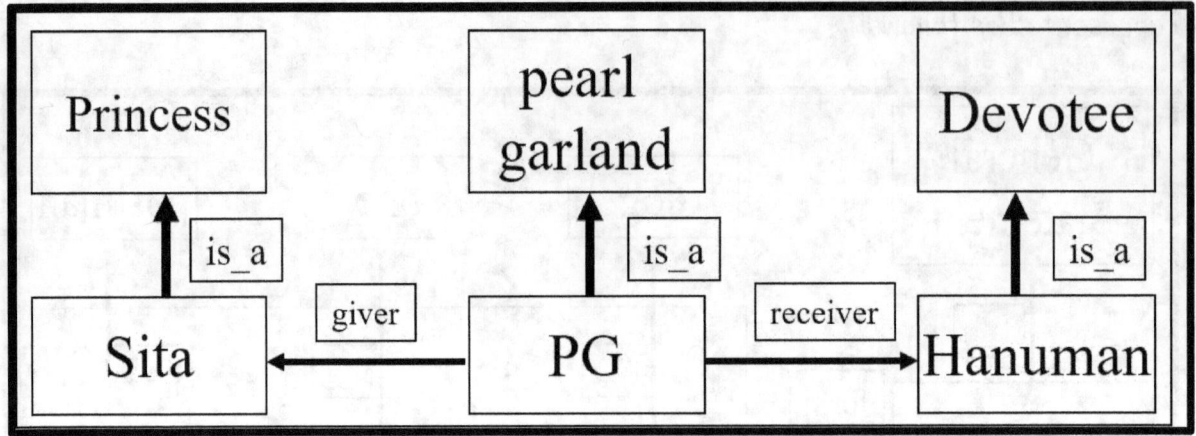

Figure 8.6: Partitioned Semantic Network (Example 5)

8.2 Frames:

A *frame* is a collection of *attributes (usually called slots) & associated values (usually called fillers)* that describe some entity in the real world.

Frames are known as *Slot-and-Filler structures*.

A *frame for a book* is given below:

Slots	Fillers
publisher	Thomson
title	Expert Systems
authors	Roosevelt, Jordan, Kevin
edition	Third
year	2016
pages	600

A filler for a slot might have a *single value as in 'publisher'* or it can have *a range of values as in 'authors'*.

Although there is no clear distinction between a semantic net & frame system, but **more structured the system is, more likely it is to be termed as a frame system**.

A single frame taken alone is rarely useful, so *we build frame systems from collections of frames* that are connected to each other.

8.2.1 Frames as Sets and Instances:

Each frame represents either a class (a set) or an instance (an element of class).

There are 2 kinds of attributes that can be associated with an instance frame:

1. Its own attributes.
2. Attributes that are inherited from the class to which it belongs.

An instance frame can override the attributes that are inherited from the class to which the instance frame belongs.

Consider the following example:

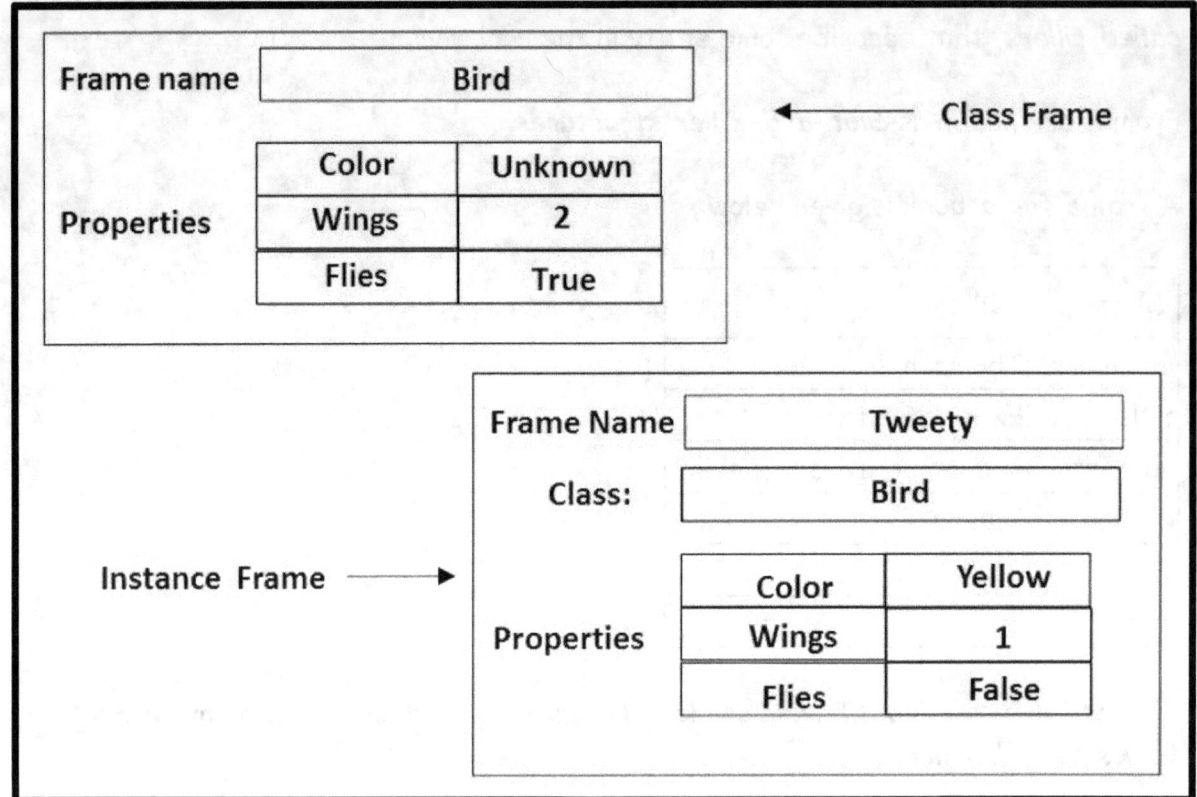

Figure 8.7: Frames as Set & Instance (Example)

Game Playing & Planning

9.1 Game Playing:

9.1.1 Overview:

Game Playing in AI refers to the development of **AI programs that can play games against a human expert**.

Charles Babbage (19th Century), Father of the Computer, thought about programming his analytical engine to play chess & later of building a machine to play tic-tac-toe.

Games are well-defined problems that generally **require intelligence to play well**.

- In game playing, the **performance of a human expert** utilizes a vast amount of **domain specific knowledge**. Such knowledge allows the human expert to generate a few promising moves for each game situation.

- In contrast, when selecting the best move, the **AI program** exploits **brute-force computational speed** to explore as many alternative moves & consequences as possible.

As the computational **speed of modern computers increases**, the **contest of knowledge versus speed** is tilting more and more in the **favor of computers**.

Game playing problems are easily solvable by **straight-forward search** from the **initial state to a goal state** (winning position). However, this is **not true for all the problems**. **Search spaces for certain problems** can turn out to be **very large**. For instance, consider the **chess problem**:

- **Branching Factor:**   35 legal moves at any given instance of time
- **Depth of the tree:**   50 moves per player
- **Search Space:** 35^{100} states

It is clear that **we need to improve the effectiveness of a search based problem**. **Two things** can be done about it:

1. Improve the **"move-generator procedure"** so that only good moves are generated.

2. Improve the "***test procedure***" so that the best move will be recognized & explored first.

To improve the ***move-generator procedure,*** we use a ***plausible-move generator*** instead of a regular one. It generates the most promising moves out of all the possible ones.

To improve the ***test procedure***, we use a ***static evolution function*** that evaluates individual board position by estimating how likely they are to eventually lead to a win. This helps in exploring the best path.

As the number of ***legal moves increases*** it becomes increasingly important in ***applying heuristics to select only the most promising moves***. The performance of overall system can be improved by adding heuristic knowledge into both ***the generator & the tester***.

9.1.2 Min-Max Search Procedure:

Min-Max is a **depth-first, depth-limited search procedure** used in game playing. The idea is to start at the current state & use the **plausible-move generator** (one that generates only good moves) to generate the set of possible successor states.

After getting the list of possible successor states, we can apply **static evolution function** to those states & choose the best one of them. Then we can trace it back to the initial state to represent the evolution of the goal state.

Assuming that the static evolution function returns large integer value for an ideal successor state, **our goal is to maximize the value of the static evolution function** for a particular state (board position). On the contrary, the **opponent's goal is to minimize the value of the static evolution function**.

The alternation of **minimizing & maximizing** the values corresponds to the opposing **strategies of the two players** & gives this method its name: **Min-Max**.

An example of **Min-Max procedure for one-ply search** is given below:

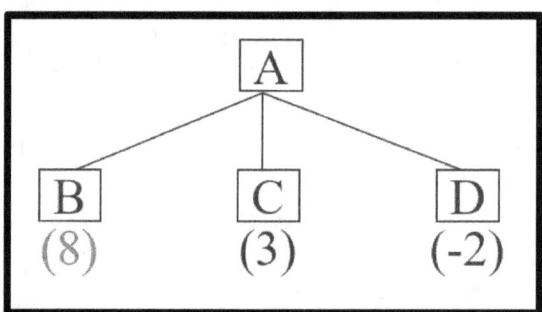

Figure 9.1: One-Ply Min-Max Search

The above example assumes a **static evolution function** that returns **values ranging from -10 to 10**, with **10 indicating a win for us, -10 indicating a win for the opponent & 0 indicating a tie situation**. Since our goal is to **maximize the value of the static evolution function**, we **select B**. Backing B's value to A, we can conclude that **A's value is 8**.

But at certain times, we would like to **implement the search for more than one-ply** (this is important in a chess game). In such case, instead of applying the static evaluation function to each of the states that we just generated, we apply the plausible-move generator to **generate a set of successor states for each state**.

If we want to stop at **two-ply search**, we apply **static evolution function** as in the following figure:

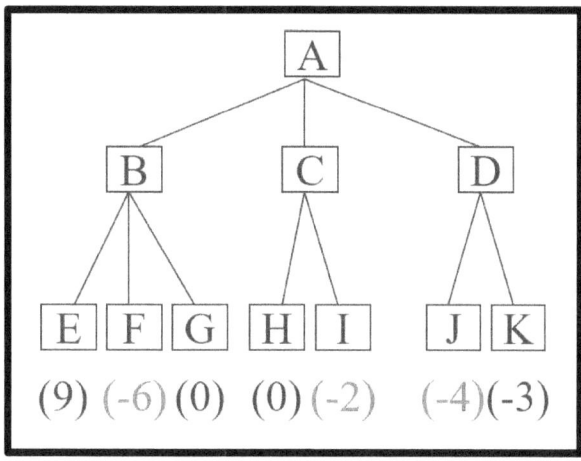

Figure 9.2: Two-Ply Min-Max Search

But now, we must consider the fact that **the opponent gets to choose which successor to choose, for backing up to previous level, in order to minimize the value of the static evolution function.**

Suppose **if we choose B**, then the **opponent gets to choose from E, F & G** in order to minimize the value of the static evolution function. In that case, the **opponent is likely to choose F** because it has the **minimum value** among the three & indicates a **win situation for the opponent**. Even though E (a successor of B) is very good for us, choosing B is not good for us because **we don't get to make the choice at this level**.

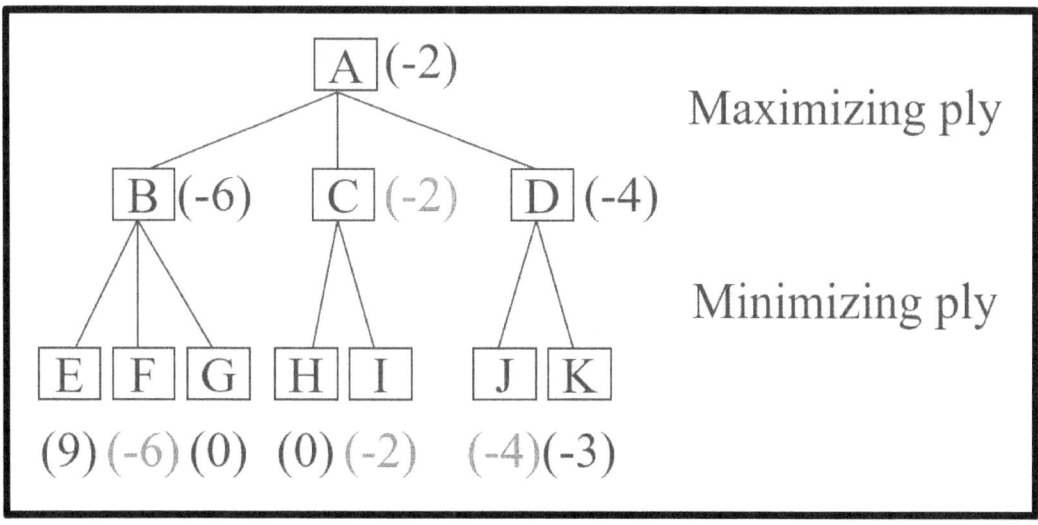

Figure 9.3: Two-Ply Min-Max Search (Backing-Up the Values)

The above figure shows the *backing up of values to the initial state*. At the level representing **opponent's choice, minimum value was chosen** & backed up. At the level representing **our choice, maximum value was chosen** & backed up.

Min-Max is a recursive procedure that relies on **two auxiliary procedures**:

1. **MOVEGEN (State, Player)** — The **plausible-move generator**, which returns a list of nodes representing the moves that can be made by Player in State.

2. **STATIC (State, Player)** — The **static evaluation function**, which returns a number representing the goodness of State from the standpoint of Player.

Limitations of Min-Max:

- One issue of Min-Max is to **decide when the recursive procedure should stop**. Various factors that influence this decision are: **either of the player has won, certain number of ply has been explored, time is up** & so on. Min-Max uses a Boolean variable called **DEEP-ENOUGH** which returns **TRUE** if search should be stopped & returns **FALSE** otherwise. It returns TRUE if the **"depth"** parameter exceeds a constant cut-off value.

- Another issue is that the **Min-Max procedure should return not one but two values: the backed-up value of the path & the path itself**. We assume that Min-Max **returns a structure** containing both the results.

Algorithm: MIN-MAX (State, Depth, Player)

1. If DEEP-ENOUGH (State, Depth), then return the structure:

   {
       VALUE = STATIC (State, Player);
       PATH = nil;
   }

   This indicates that there are no further successors of this State & its value is the one that's determined by the static evaluation function.

2. Else, generate one more ply of the tree by calling MOVE-GEN (State, Player) & set SUCCESSOR to the list which the function returns.

3. If SUCCESSOR is empty, then there are no moves to be made, so return the same structure as mentioned in step 1.

4. If SUCCESSOR is not empty, then examine each element & keep track of the best one. This is done as follows:

   Initialize BEST-SCORE to the minimum value that STATIC can return. For each element SUCC of SUCCESSOR, do the following:

   4.1. Set RESULT-SUCC to MIN-MAX (SUCC, Depth + 1, OPPOSITE(Player))
        This will explore SUCC

   4.2. Set NEW-VALUE to VALUE (RESULT-SUCC)

   4.3. If NEW-VALUE > BEST-SCORE, then we have found a successor that is better than any that have been examined so far. Record this data:

      4.3.1.   Set BEST-SCORE to NEW-VALUE
      4.3.2.   Set BEST-PATH to PATH (RESULT-SUCC)

5. Return the structure:

   {
        VALUE = BEST-SCORE;
        PATH = BEST-PATH;
   }

9.1.3 Alpha-beta Pruning:

As **Min-Max** is a **depth first search**, a **particular path is explored until time permits**. The **static evolution function** is applied to the states at the **last step of the path**.

The **efficiency of the depth first search can be improved** by using branch & bound technique in which **partial solutions that are worse than the known solutions can be abandoned early**. This modified strategy of Min-Max search is known as **alpha-beta pruning**.

It requires to maintain two threshold values:

> *Alpha*: the one representing **a lower bound**.
> *Beta*: the one representing **an upper bound**.

Instead of referring to alpha and beta, Min-Max uses two values, **USE-THRESH & PASS-THRESH**. **USE-THRESH** is used to compute cutoffs. **PASS-THRESH** is passed to next level as its **USE-THRESH**.

Algorithm: MIN-MAX-A-B (State, Depth, Player, USE-THRESH, PASS-THRESH)

1. If DEEP-ENOUGH (State, Depth), then return the structure:

   {
       VALUE = STATIC (State, Player);
       PATH = nil;
   }

   This indicates that there are no further successors of this State & its value is the one that's determined by the static evaluation function.

2. Else, generate one more ply of the tree by calling MOVE-GEN (State, Player) & set SUCCESSOR to the list which the function returns.

3. If SUCCESSOR is empty, then there are no moves to be made, so return the same structure as mentioned in step 1.

> 4. If SUCCESSOR is not empty, then examine each element & keep track of the best one. This is done as follows:
>
> each element SUCC of SUCCESSOR, do the following:
>
> 4.1. Set RESULT-SUCC to MIN-MAX-A-B (SUCC, Depth + 1, OPPOSITE(Player), PASS-THRESH, USE-THRESH)
>
> This will explore SUCC
>
> 4.2. Set NEW-VALUE to VALUE (RESULT-SUCC)
>
> 4.3. If NEW-VALUE > PASS-THRESH, then we have found a successor that is better than any that have been examined so far. Record this data:
>
> 4.3.1. Set PASS-THRESH to NEW-VALUE
> 4.3.2. Set BEST-PATH to PATH (RESULT-SUCC)
>
> 5. Return the structure:
>
> {
>   VALUE = PASS-THRESH;
>   PATH = BEST-PATH;
> }

To see how the **alpha-beta pruning** works, consider the following **example**:

Considering the following figure, after examining the nodes D & E, we know that the value of B will be 3 (as it is a minimizing ply).

Similarly, after examining the nodes F & G, we realize that the value of G is unknown. But we know the value of F. We can deduce that regardless of the value of G, the value of C will be less than or equal to -5 (as it is a minimizing ply).

Now, comparing the values of B & C, we can deduce that the value of A will be 3 (as it is a maximizing ply).

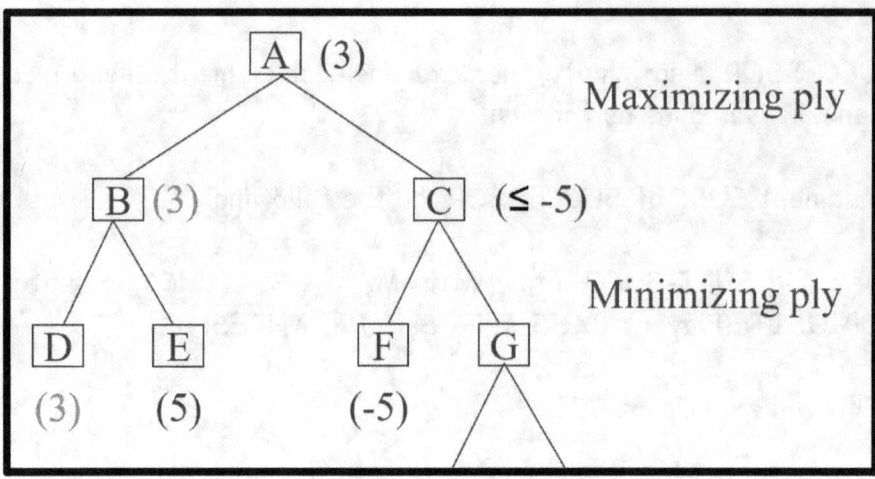

Figure 9.4: Min-Max Search with Alpha-Beta Pruning

We'll never need to explore the node G. Thus, *even if G could be explored up to three more ply, we'll eliminate that process, in turn reducing the complexity of the search.*

9.1.4 Examples:

9.1.4.1 Example 1:

Consider the following 2 player game tree in which static scores are given from the first player's point of view:

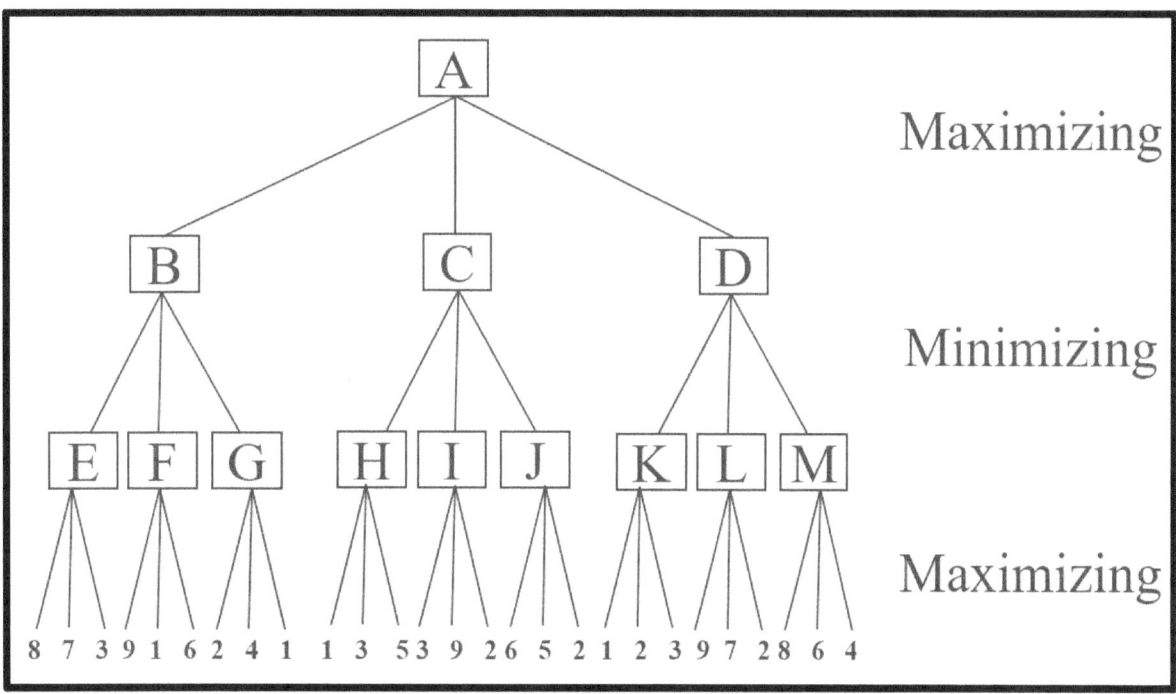

Figure 9.5: Min-Max Search (Example 1)

Suppose the first player is the maximizing player. What move should be chosen? Why? Use Mini-Max search to solve. Also explain limitations of Min-Max search. How to overcome them?

Limitations of Min-Max & how to Overcome them:

- One issue of Min-Max is to **decide when the recursive procedure should stop**. Various factors that influence this decision are: **either of the player has won, certain number of ply has been explored, time is up** & so on. Min-Max uses a Boolean variable called **DEEP-ENOUGH** which returns **TRUE** if search should be stopped & returns **FALSE** otherwise. It returns TRUE if the **"depth"** parameter exceeds a constant cut-off value.

> Another issue is that the **Min-Max procedure should return not one but two values: the backed-up value of the path & the path itself**. We assume that Min-Max **returns a structure** containing both the results.

Solution using Min-Max search:

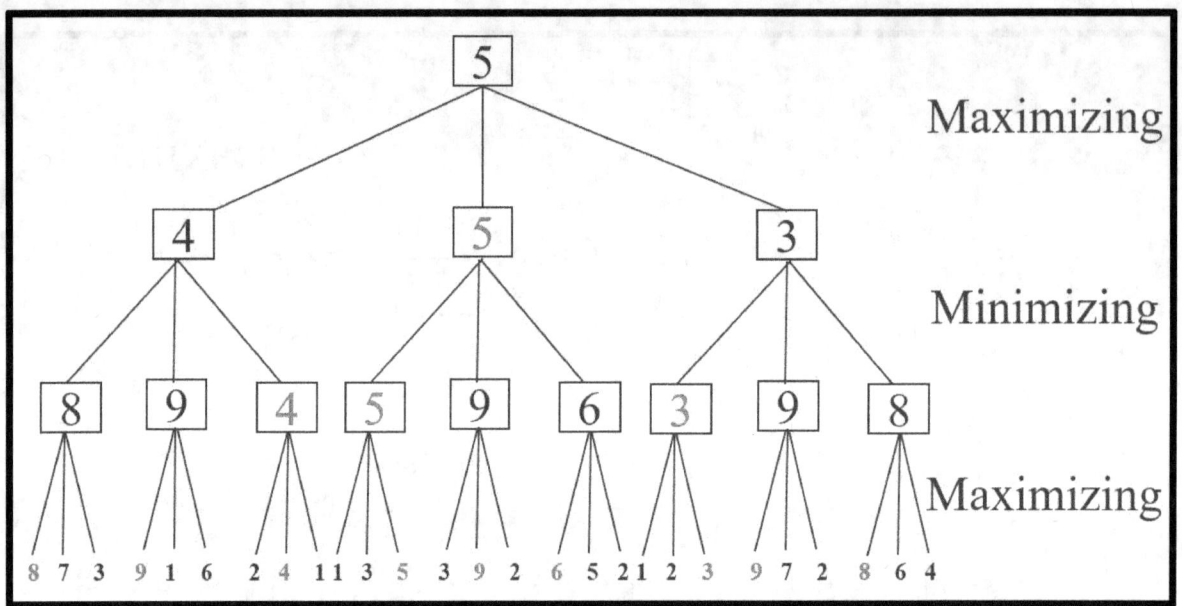

Figure 9.6: Min-Max Search (Example 1) (Solution)

Thus, C should be chosen from A.

9.1.4.2 Example 2:

Consider the following game tree in which static scores are given from the first player's point of view:

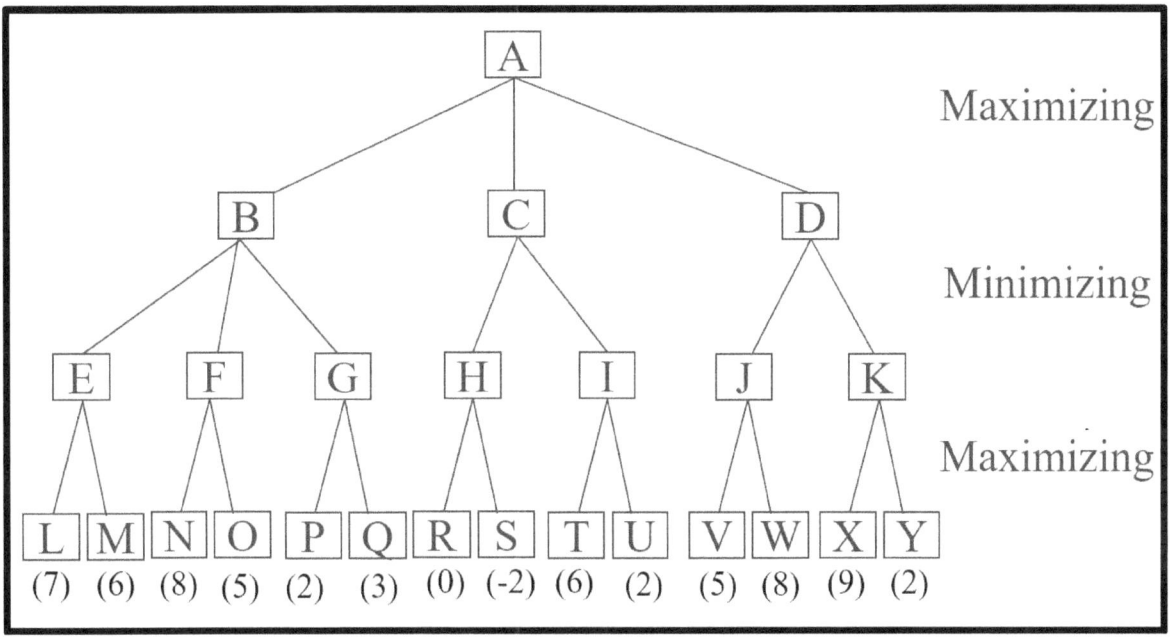

Figure 9.7: Min-Max Search (Example 2)

Suppose the first player is maximizing player. Applying mini-max search, show the backed-up values in the tree. What move will the MAX choose? If the nodes are expanded from left to right, what nodes would not be visited using alpha-beta pruning.

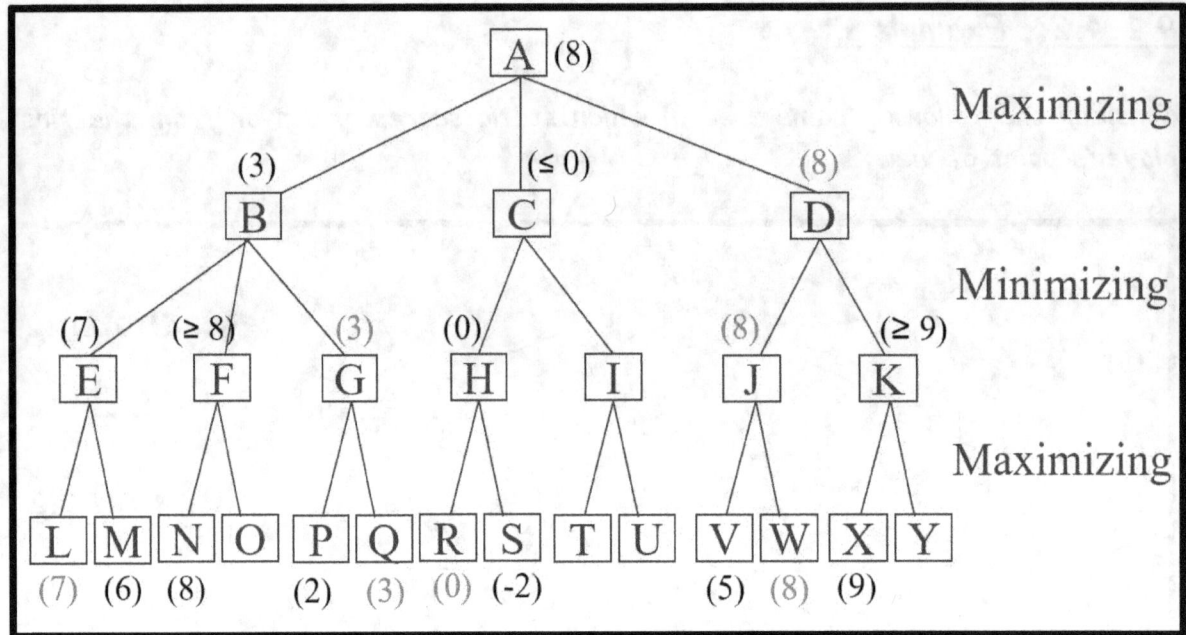

Figure 9.8: Min-Max Search (Example 2) (Solution)

The backed-up values are given in the above figure.

MAX will choose D from A.

The nodes that will not be visited due to alpha-beta pruning are O, I, T, U & Y.

9.1.4.3 Example 3:

'Minimax is not good for game playing when the opponent is not playing optimally'. Justify using suitable example.

Let us consider that the opponent is supposed to minimize the value of the static evolution function. If the opponent is not playing optimally, he might not select the minimum value from the choices & thus, might manipulate us in to thinking the particular path is optimal. But in reality, it is not the optimal path.

Consider the following example:

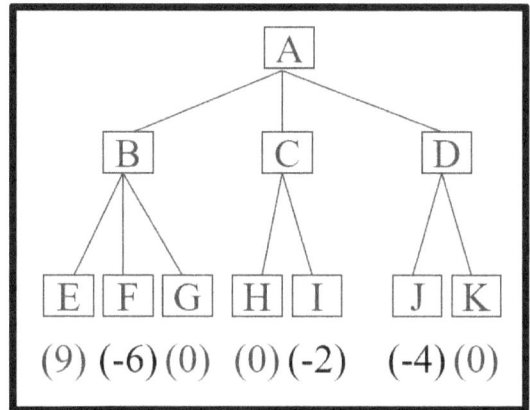

Figure 9.9: Min-Max Search (Example 3)

Following would have been the solution if the opponent played optimally:

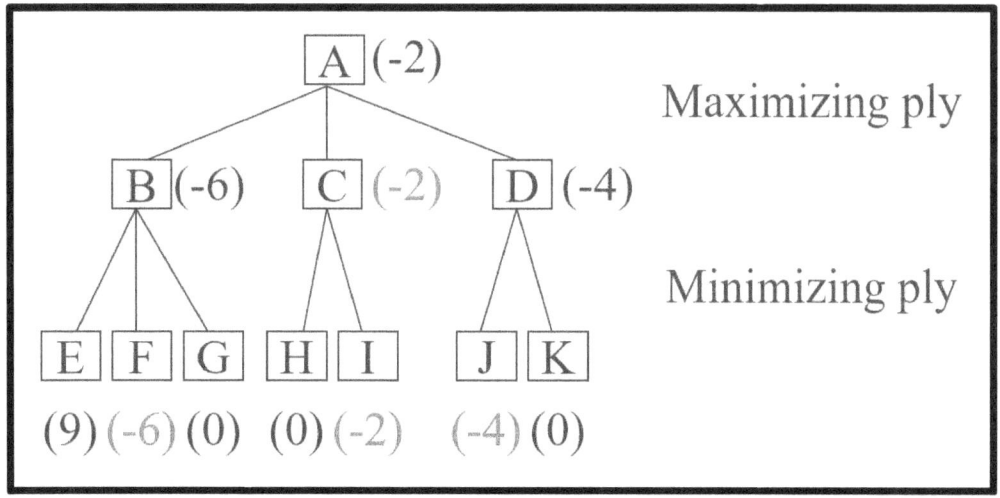

Figure 9.10: Min-Max Search (Example 3) (Ideal Solution)

But let's consider a case where the opponent does not play optimally. Let us see what will be the solution if the opponent selects the value 0 instead of -4 while evaluating nodes J & K.

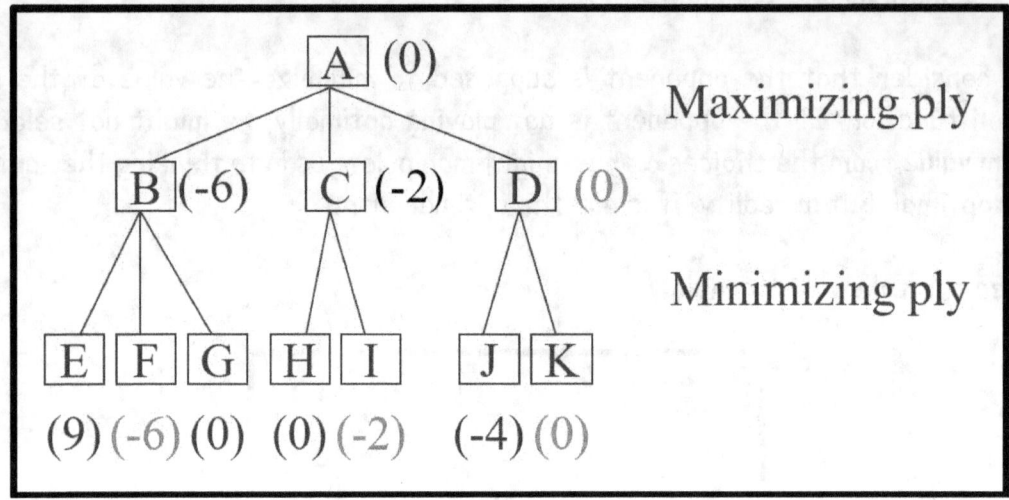

Figure 9.11: Min-Max Search (Example 3) (Flawed Solution)

As seen in the above figure, the solution might completely change if the opponent does not play optimally.

The ideal path for the above example is A-C-I with the value of A being (-2). But if the opponent does not play optimally, the path changes to A-D-K with value of A being (0).

Thus, we can say that *'Minimax is not good for game playing when the opponent is not playing optimally'*.

9.2 Planning:

Often, we come across AI problems that are too big to be solved individually. For such problem, it is important to be able to work on small pieces of the problem separately & then to combine the partial solutions into a complete problem solution. For this, we use *Planning*.

Planning techniques are problem-solving methods that rely heavily on problem *decomposition*.

9.2.1 An Example Domain - The Blocks World:

Planning techniques that we are about to discuss can be applied on a wide variety of task domains. The **blocks world** is such a domain. There is **a flat surface on which blocks can be placed**. There are a number of **square blocks, all the same size**. They **can be stacked up on one another**. There is a **robot arm** that can **manipulate the blocks**. The **actions it can perform** include:

- **UNSTACK (A, B)** — Pick up block A from its current position (on block B). The arm must be empty and block A must have no blocks on top of it.

- **STACK (A, B)** — Place block A on block B. The arm must already be holding block A and the surface of B must be clear.

- **PICKUP (A)** — Pick up block A from the table & hold it. The arm must be empty & there must be nothing on top of block A.

- **PUTDOWN (A)** — Put block A down on the table. The arm must have been holding block A.

Note that in the problem that we just described, the robotic arm can hold only one block at a time. Also, each block can have at most one other block directly on top of it.

To specify both these conditions, *following predicates can be used*:

- **ON (A, B)** — Block A is on block B.

- **ONTABLE (A)** — Block A is on the table.
- **CLEAR (A)** — There is nothing on top of block A.
- **HOLDING (A)** — The arm is holding block A.
- **ARMEMPTY** — The arm is holding nothing.

Various logical statements can be true in this problem. For example, *if the arm is holding anything, it can't be empty*. It can be represented as follows:

$$\exists x: HOLDING(x) \rightarrow \neg ARMEMPTY$$

9.2.2 Components of a Planning System:

A **planning system** is a problem-solving technique that **decomposes a large problem into smaller subproblems, works on the subproblems separately, & then combines the partial solutions to form a complete solution.**

It is necessary to perform the following **five functions for implementation of an effective planning system**:

1. **Choose the best rule to apply next**, based on the best available heuristic information.

2. **Apply the chosen rule to compute the new problem state** that arises from its application.

3. **Detect when a solution has been found**.

4. **Detect dead ends so that they can be abandoned** & the system's effort can be directed in more promising directions.

5. **Detect when a nearly correct solution has been found & use special techniques to make it totally correct**.

9.2.3 Goal Stack Planning:

Goal Stack Planning is a **planning technique** in which the **system makes use of a single stack** (known as **goal stack**) that **contains both goals & the operators** that have been proposed to satisfy those goals.

The system also relies on a **database that describes the current situation & a set of operators**.

The **goal stack planning** method primarily **solves problems that have conjoined goals**, by **solving one goal at a time, in a sequence**. A plan generated by this technique first **attains the first goal, followed by the second goal & so on**. At any given step of the problem-solving process, **the top goal on the stack will be pursued**.

When a sequence of operators that satisfies a goal, is found, that sequence is applied to the state, yielding new state. Next, the goal that is then at the top of the stack is explored & solved. This process continues until the goal stack is empty. Then as one last check, the original goal is compared to the final state derived. If any components of the goal are not satisfied in that state, then those unsolved parts of the goal are reinserted onto the stack and the process is resumed.

To understand how the process works, let's consider the following **Blocks world example** & solve it **using goal stack planning**:

Figure 9.12: Goal Stack Planning (Blocks World)

Initial state can be described as follows:
ON (B, A) ∧ ONTABLE (A) ∧ ONTABLE (C) ∧ ONTABLE (D) ∧ ARMEMPTY

Goal state can be described as:
ON (C, A) ∧ ON (B, D) ∧ ONTABLE (A) ∧ ONTABLE (D)

Initially, **Goal Stack is equivalent to the Goal State**. We then **divide the problem into four subproblems**.

Two of which are already solved: ONTABLE (A)
                                                 ONTABLE (D)

The other two can be solved using either of the following approaches:

1. ON (C, A)

    ON (B, D)
    ON (C, A) ∧ ON (B, D) ∧ ONTABLE (A) ∧ ONTABLE (D)

2. ON (B, D)

    ON (C, A)
    ON (C, A) ∧ ON (B, D) ∧ ONTABLE (A) ∧ ONTABLE (D)

The *method used* is:

- ➢ ***Investigate the first node on the goal stack***, i.e. the top goal.

- ➢ If a ***sequence of operators*** is found that ***satisfies this goal***, then the ***goal is removed from the goal stack*** & the ***next goal is attempted***.

- ➢ This ***continues until the goal state is empty***.

Chapter 10

Natural Language Processing

10.1 Introduction to Natural Language Processing:

Language is meant for communicating. If we succeed at building a **computational model of language**, we'll have a **powerful tool for communicating** about the world.

So far, the **largest part of human communication** occurs in the **form of speech**. **Written language is fairly recent invention & plays a less significant role in communication**. However, **processing written language is easier** as compared to speech processing.

The problem of **Natural Language Processing (NLP)** can be divided into two tasks:

- **Processing written text**, using lexical, syntactic & semantic knowledge of the language.

- **Processing spoken language**, using
    - All the **information needed to process text**.
    - Additional knowledge about **phonology**.
    - Added **information to handle the ambiguities** that arise in speech.

Phases involved in Natural Language Processing (NLP) are as follows:

1. **Morphological (Structural) Analysis:** Individual words are analyzed into their components & non-word tokens such as punctuation are separated from the words. Consider the following sentence:

    I want to print Bill's .init file.

    Morphological analysis on the above sentence must do two things:

    a. Pull a proper noun *"Bill"* from the word *"Bill's"*.
    b. Recognize the sequence *".init"* as a file extension.

2. **Syntactic Analysis (Parsing):** This phase uses the result of morphological analysis phase to transform the linear sequences of words into **hierarchical**

structures that shows the relation between those words. The hierarchical structure for the sentence **"I want to print Bill's .init file."** is as follows:

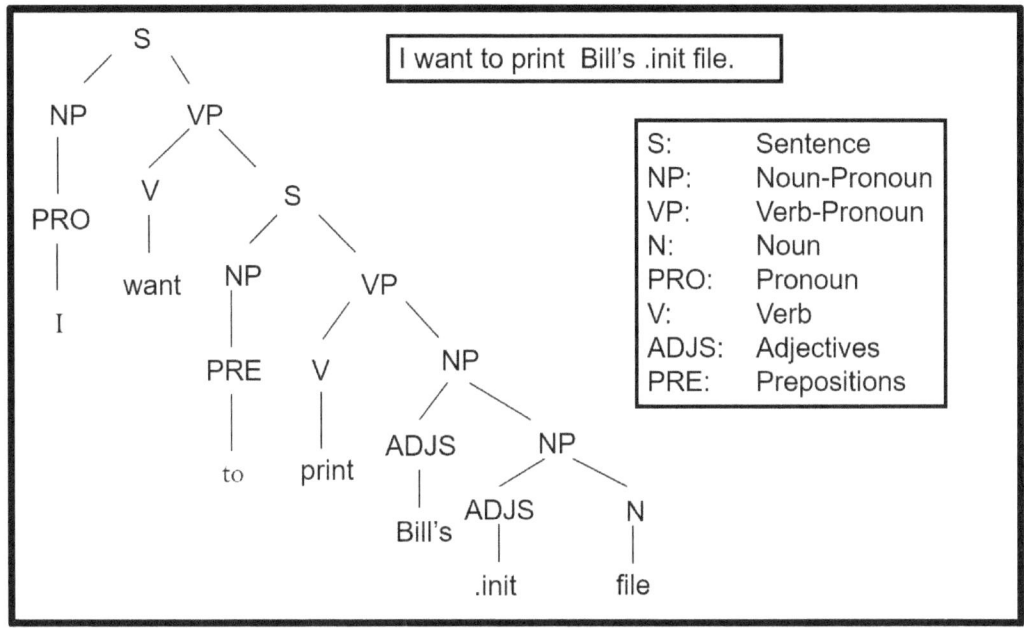

Figure 10.1: Syntactic Analysis – Natural Language Processing (Example 1)

3. **Semantic Analysis**: The structures created by the syntactic analyzer are assigned **meanings**. A mapping is made between the syntactic structures & objects in the task domain. The words in the structure are mapped to the appropriate objects in the knowledge base. The hierarchical structure is then updated to correspond to the actual meaning of the sentence. Structures for which no mapping is possible may be rejected.

4. **Discourse (Extended) integration**: The meaning of an individual sentence may depend on the sentences that precede it & may influence the meanings of the sentences that follow it. For instance, consider the sentence: **"I want to print Bill's .init file."** Here, we do not know whom the pronoun **"I"** or the noun **"Bill"** refers to. To identify these references, we need to relate it to the current discourse context. Once the correct referent for Bill is known, we can determine which file is being referred to.

5. **Pragmatic (Practical) Analysis**: We now have a complete description of what was said. Now we need to **decide what to display as a result**. For certain sentences, whose **intent is clearly declarative**, we can simple **record what was said & show it as an output**. But for some sentences whose **intended effect is**

different than what was said, the structure representing ***what was said is reinterpreted to determine what was actually meant***. This ***reinterpretation can be done by applying a set of rules that characterize dialogues***.

10.2 Syntactic Processing:

Syntactic processing is the step of NLP in which the **input sentence is converted into a hierarchical structure**. This is known as **Parsing**. Most **parsing systems** have the following **two components**:

1. <u>Grammar:</u> A declarative **representation of the syntactic facts about the language**.

2. <u>Parser:</u> A **procedure** that **compares the grammar with the input sentences** to produce **parsed hierarchical structures**, also known as **Parse Tree**.

The most common way to **represent grammars** is as a **set of production rules**. Following is an example of **grammar for a fragment of English language**:

$S \rightarrow NP\ VP$
$NP \rightarrow the\ NP1\ |\ PRO\ |\ PN\ |\ NP1$
$NP1 \rightarrow ADJS\ |\ N$
$ADJS \rightarrow \epsilon\ |\ ADJ\ ADJS$
$VP \rightarrow V\ |\ V\ NP$
$N \rightarrow file\ |\ printer$
$PN \rightarrow Bill$
$PRO \rightarrow I$
$ADJ \rightarrow short\ |\ long\ |\ fast$
$V \rightarrow printed\ |\ created\ |\ want$

Using the above grammar, we can generate a parse tree for a given input. Following is the **parse tree** for the sentence: *"Bill printed the file"*

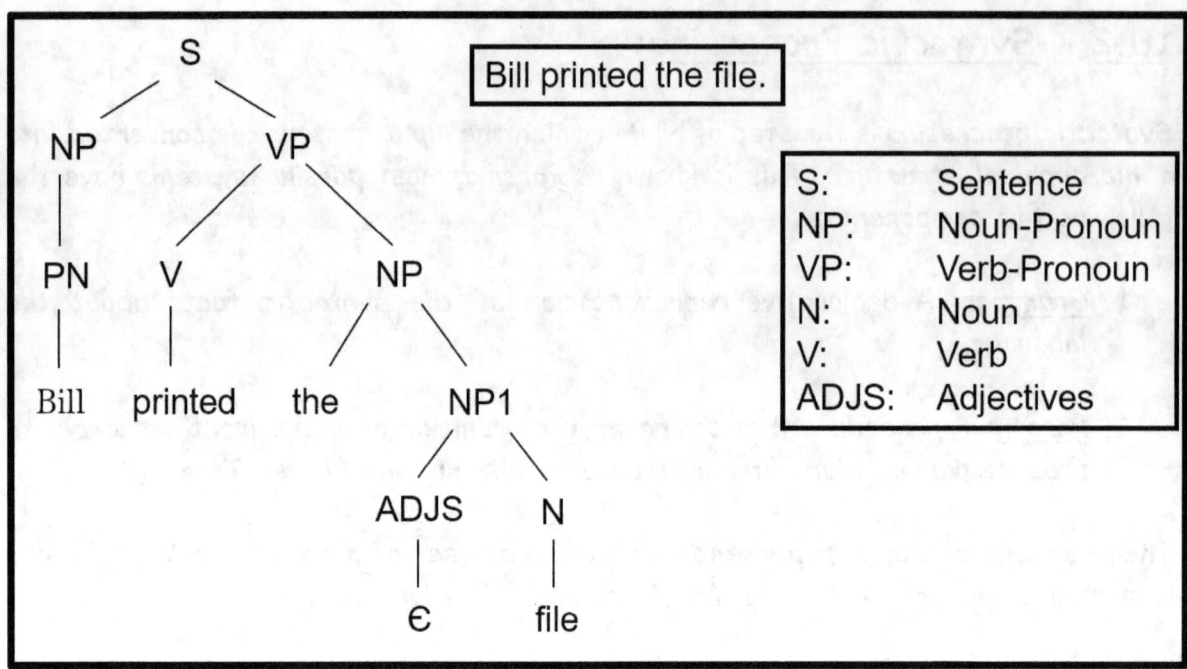

Figure 10.2: Syntactic Analysis - Natural Language Processing (Example 2)

10.3 Semantic Processing:

Generating a parse tree is just the beginning of the process of understanding language. We must generate the **representation for the meaning of the sentence**. Since **understanding is a mapping process**, we must **first define the target language** to which we are trying **to map the input**.

There is **no single target language** that has the capability to **map all possible sentences**. The **choice of target language** depends on **what is to be done with the meanings once they are constructed**. **Two major target languages used in NLP** are as follows:

1. When **input language is considered as a phenomenon on its own**, for example when one builds a program whose goal is to read text & answer questions about it, target language can be designed specifically to support language processing.

2. When **input language is being used as an interface to another program**, then the target language must be an input to that other program. Thus, the design of the target language is driven by that other program to which the input has to be fed.

After the **target language has been defined**, we can **generate semantic grammars** for the target language. Then the **meaning of the input can be determined by performing semantic actions** on the input based on the **semantic grammar**.

10.4 Discourse & Pragmatic Processing:

To understand a given sentence, it is necessary to consider the discourse (extensive) & pragmatic (practical) context in which the sentence was said.

Consider the following relationships that might exist between words in the sentence & their discourse context:

1. **Identical Entities**:

    - Jim had a black car.
    - Joseph liked it.
    - The word "it" should be identified as referring to black car.

2. **Parts of Entities**:

    - Jim went to his office.
    - The chair was missing.
    - The phrase "chair" should be recognized as an entity that belonged to Jim's office.

3. **Parts of Actions**:

    - Jim went to his office.
    - He bought flowers on the way.
    - Buying flowers should be considered as a part of going to office.

4. **Entities Involved in Actions**:

    - There was a robbery at Jim's office.
    - They took the Macintosh.
    - The pronoun "they" should refer to the robbers.

5. **Elements of Sets**:

    - The cars that Jim owned were Ferrari, Mustang & Porsche.
    - He sold the Porsche.
    - Porsche means the Porsche car.

6. **_Names of Individuals_:**

    ➢ Jim went to the movies.

7. **_Causal Chain_:**

    ➢ There was a big snow storm yesterday.
    ➢ The schools were closed today.

To understand the language effectively, it is necessary to understand all of the above-mentioned relationships that might exist between words in the sentence & their discourse context.

Connectionist Models

11.1 Introduction: Hopfield Networks

A *neural network* (also known as *connectionist network*) is an *AI technique that mimics the operation of the human brain* & comprises of densely connected group of *neuron-like processing units* that *works parallelly*.

Dr. John Hopfield, in *1982*, proposed a neural network to store & retrieve memory like the human brain. It is known as *Hopfield Network* & has the following characteristics:

> *Distributed Representation*: A memory is stored as a *pattern of activation across a set of neurons* (processing elements). *Memories can be superimposed on one another*, that is, *different memories* can be represented by *different patterns* over the same *set of neurons*.

> *Distributed, Asynchronous Control*: Each *neuron makes decisions based only on its own local situation*. All these local actions add up to a global solution.

> *Content-Addressable Memory*: A number of patterns can be stored in a network. To *retrieve a pattern*, we need *only specify a portion of it*. The network automatically finds the closest match.

> *Fault Tolerance*: If a *few neurons misbehave or fail* completely, the *network will still function* properly.

In a *simple Hopfield network*, a *neuron* either is ON (+1) (active) or OFF (-1) (inactive). The *state of a neuron (ON or OFF) will be renewed depending on the input it receives from other neurons*.

Every neuron in a Hopfield network is fully connected to every other neuron in the network.

A *Hopfield network* is *initially trained to store a number of patterns or memories*. It is then able to *recognize any of the learned patterns by exposure to only partial information* about that pattern.

Following figure shows a *simple Hopfield network*:

Artificial Intelligence

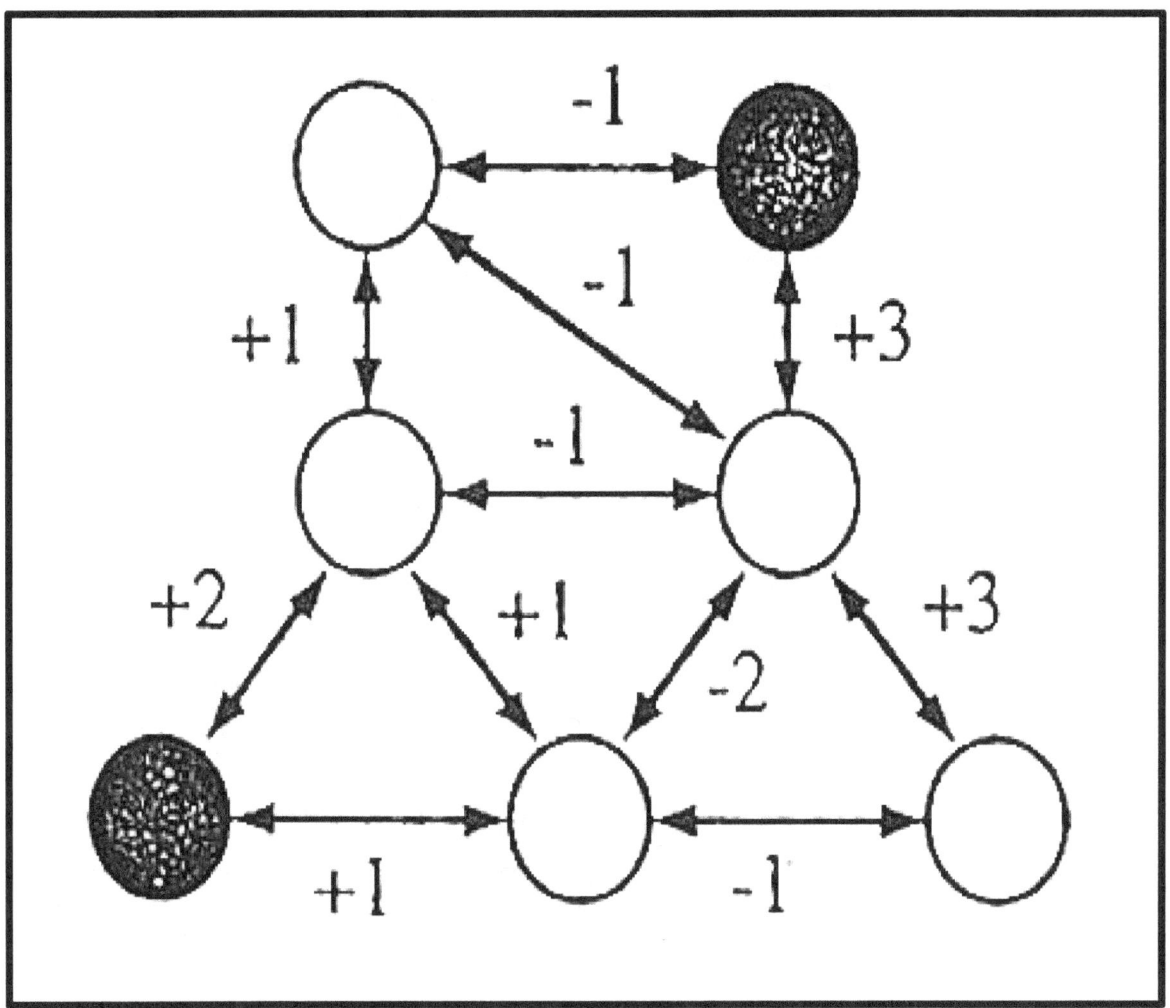

Figure 11.1: A Simple Hopfield Network

The **black neurons represent ON state** & the **white ones represent OFF state**.

Neurons are connected to each other with **weighted connection**.

> A **positive weighted connection** indicates that the **two neurons tend to activate each other**.

> Whereas a **negative weighted connection** indicates that **an activated neuron has the capability to deactivate the neighboring neuron**.

Considering the above two properties, if we perform a **series of activations on the Hopfield network** shown in the above figure, we get the **following stable states**:

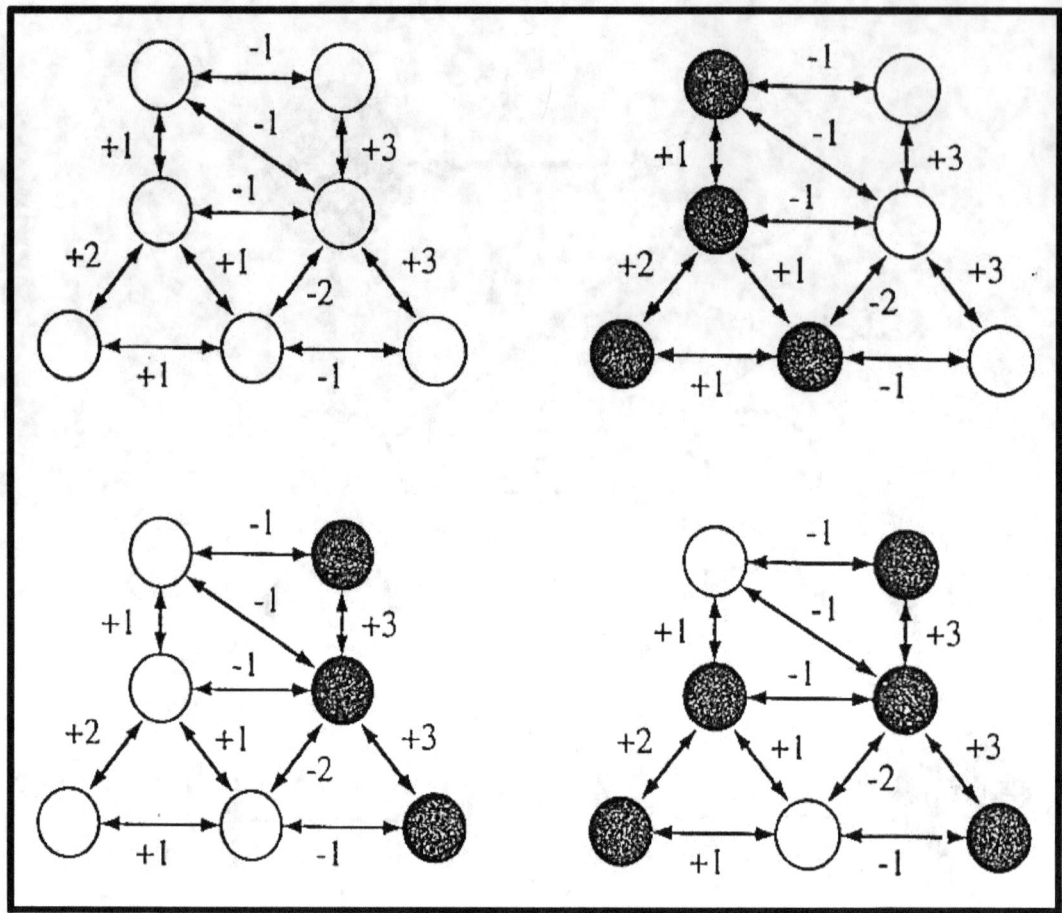

Figure 11.2: Stable States of a Particular Hopfield Network

That is, **for any given initial state, if we perform a series of activations, this particular Hopfield network will settle into one of the above four stable configurations**.

The **operation of a Hopfield network** is termed as <u>Parallel relaxation</u>. The **algorithm for parallel relaxation** on a **Hopfield network** is as follows:

<u>Parallel Relaxation Algorithm</u>:

1. If current state of the network is unstable, choose a random neuron (N). Else return SUCCESS.

2. If any of the neighbors of N are active, computes the sum of the weights on the connections to those active neighbors. Else go to step 1.

3. If the sum is positive, the unit becomes active, else it becomes inactive.

11.2 Artificial Neural Networks:

An *artificial neural network* is an *interconnected network of nodes* that process the information in the *same way as biological neural networks* (e.g. *Human brain*).

Neural networks resemble the *human brain* in the following two ways:

- A neural network *acquires knowledge through learning.*
- A neural network's *knowledge is stored in the form of inter-neuron connection (link) strengths* known as *synaptic weights*.

To understand the functioning of an *artificial neural network*, let us first consider the following *structure of a biological neuron*:

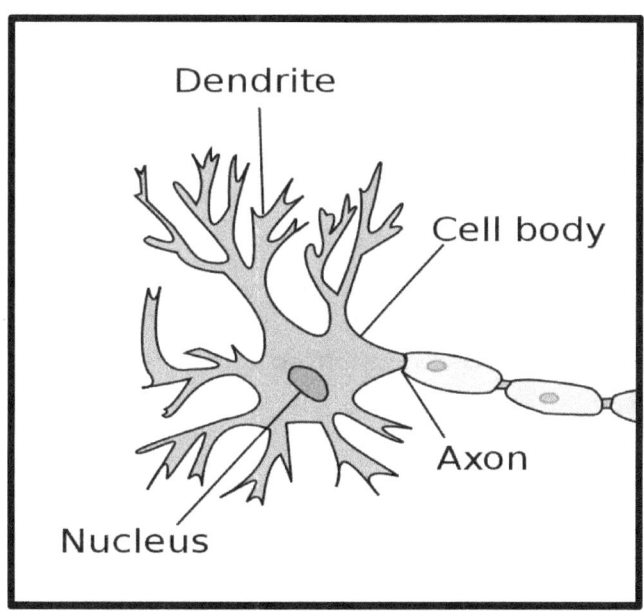

Figure 11.3: A Biological Neuron

Typically, a *biological neuron* contains three important parts:

- *A cell body* that directs all activities of the neuron.

- *Dendrites*, which are short fibers that receive messages from other neurons and forward those messages to the cell body

- *The axon*, a long single fiber that transmits messages from the cell body to dendrites of other neurons.

Now let us consider *a neuron that exists in an artificial neural network*:

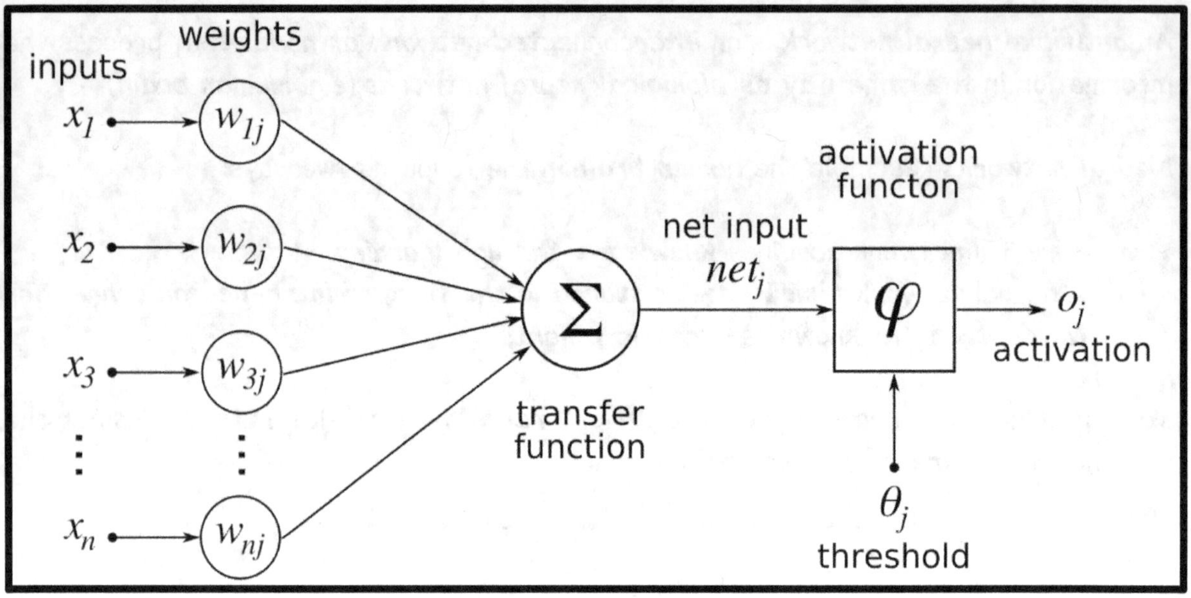

Figure 11.4: An Artificial Neuron

An *artificial neuron works in the following manner*:

- It receives a **series of input (x_1, x_2, ..., x_n) from its neighboring neurons**. These inputs are received through the **weighted connection that the neuron has with its neighbors**. These **weighted links** are equivalent to **Dendrites in a biological neuron**.

- The inputs are **collected by a transfer function that performs the summation of the inputs**. Each **input is multiplied by its corresponding weight**. Typically, the **weight represents the strength of the connection between neurons** in the network.

- After summing up the inputs, the **transfer function sends the net input to an activation function**. The **transfer function** is equivalent to **Cell Body in a biological neuron**.

- The **value of net input** can range anywhere **from zero to infinity**. To limit this value, a threshold is set. Depending on the **net input value**, the **activation function** performs the **activation**. This is similar to **Axon in a biological neuron**.

Various types of activation functions are discussed in the next section.

11.3 Activation Functions:

A *neuron* in an *artificial neural network* is an *information processing unit* that tries to *mimic the operation of biological neurons* (as the one in a human brain).

An *activation function* is a part of the *neuron* that is used to *get desired output based on the input*. The *value of input* can range from *zero to infinity*, so to *limit the value of the output* of the neuron, a *threshold* is set. Using this threshold value, the *activation function limits the value of the output of the neuron*.

The normalized range of the output of neuron is considered to be [0,1] or [-1,1].

There are several types of activation functions. Few of them are discussed below::

1. **Threshold Activation Function (Step Function):**

    Here, *if the value of the net input is above a certain value (threshold), the function activates the neuron*. If it's less than the threshold, it doesn't activate the neuron. The *value '1' represents the activated state & '0' represents deactivated state*. In the following case, the value of threshold is 0.

    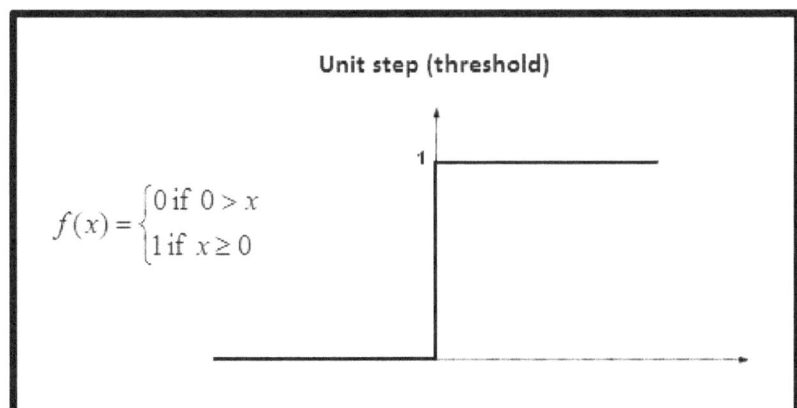

    Figure 11.5: Threshold Activation Function

2. **Linear Activation Function:**

    The problem with *step function* is that it can *only be used to create a binary system* that says YES or NO. It *can't create a system that gives a range of output*. To do that, we introduce *Linear Activation Function*.
    Linear Activation Function is a *straight-line function* where *activation is proportional to the input* & is *not binary*. However, we have an *upper threshold*

& a **lower threshold**. I the value of input is greater than upper threshold, it is considered as 1 & if it is less than the lower threshold, it is considered as 0. *Any value between the threshold range is normalized to be presented as it is.*

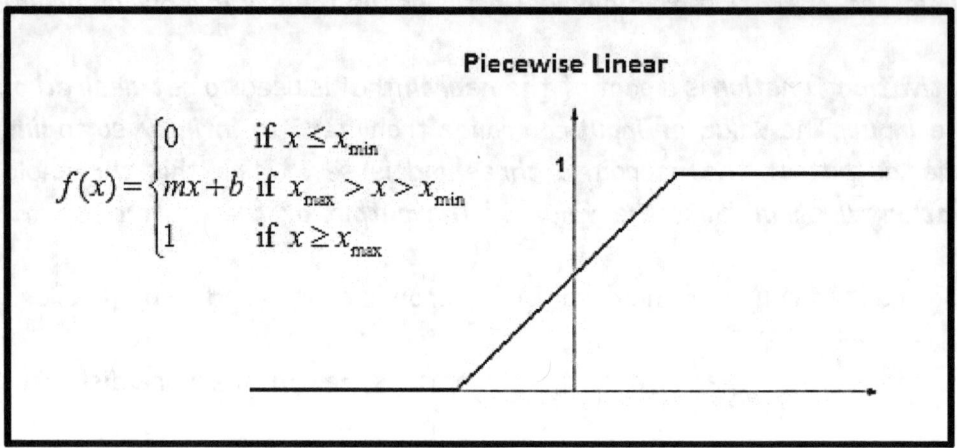

Figure 11.6: Linear Activation Function

3. **Sigmoid Function:**

The **sigmoid function** is the most common form of activation function used in the construction of artificial neural networks. Whereas a threshold function assumes the value of 0 or 1, a **sigmoid function assumes a continuous range of values form 0 to 1**.

$$f(x) = \frac{1}{1 + e^{(-x)}}$$

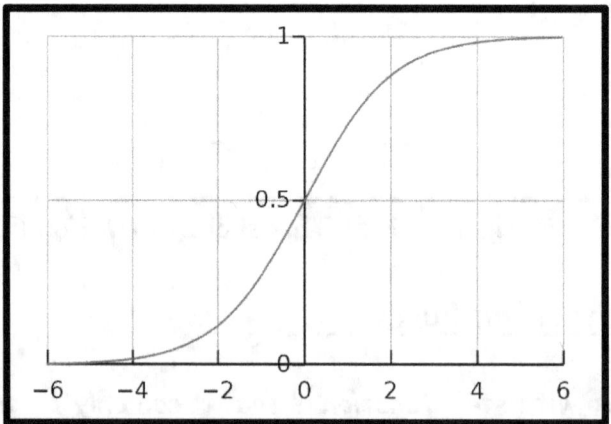

Figure 11.7: Sigmoid Activation Function

11.4 Application of Neural Networks:

- **_Classification_**: A neural network can be trained to classify given pattern or data set into predefined class.

- **_Prediction_**: A neural network can be trained to produce outputs that are expected from given input. This can be done by evaluating historical data patterns. E.g. Weather prediction.

- **_Clustering_**: A Neural network can be used to identify a special characteristic of the data & classify them into different categories without any prior knowledge of data.

- **_Pattern Recognition_**: A neural network can be used to recognize vision. speech & handwriting. It finds its application in areas such digital signal verification, text-to-speech conversion, optical text reading & so on.

11.5 Learning in Neural Networks:

11.5.1 Perceptron:

The **perceptron** was one of the earliest **neural network models**. It models a neuron by taking a **weighted sum of its inputs** & sending the **output 1 if the sum is greater than a predefined threshold value**, else it sends the output 0.

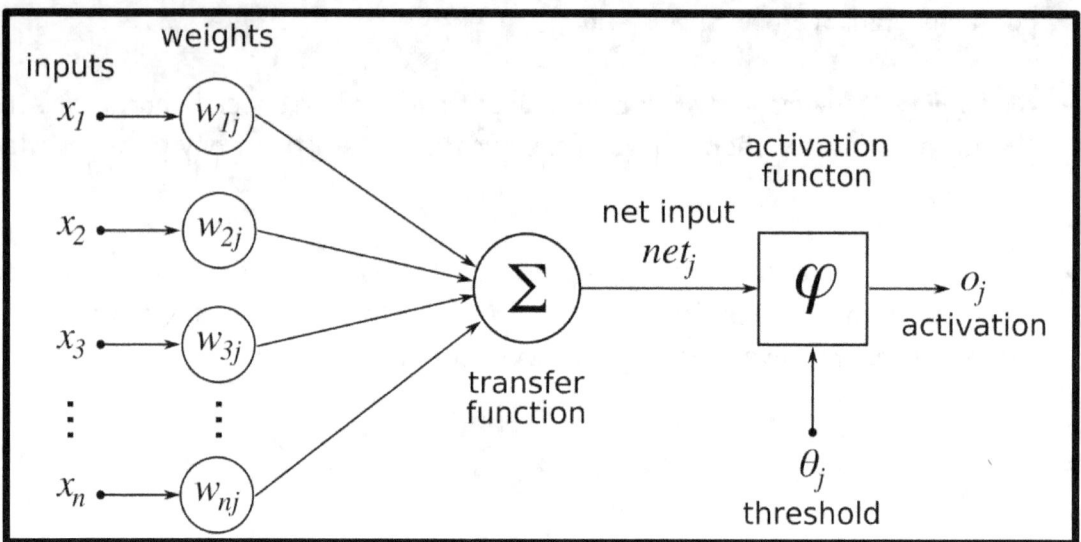

Figure 11.8: Perceptron

A **perceptron works in the following manner**:

- It receives a **series of input** (x_1, x_2, ..., x_n) **from its neighboring neurons**. These inputs are received through the **weighted connection that the neuron has with its neighbors**.

- The inputs are **collected by a transfer function that performs the summation of the inputs**. Each **input is multiplied by its corresponding weight**. Typically, the **weight represents the strength of the connection between neurons** in the network.

- After summing up the inputs, the **transfer function sends the net input to an activation function**.

- The **activation function** sends output 1 if the net input is greater than a predefined threshold value, else it sends the output 0.

Normally, the **weight assigned to the connections between neurons shows the tendency of the perceptron to fire irrespective of its input**. But for **certain problems such as the classification problem**, we need the **perceptron to fire only when the input falls into a certain category**. To do so, we use **Learning process** on the perceptron.

Learning is the process of **modifying the weight values & the threshold values** in a way that the **perceptron gives the desired output**. Following is a schematic diagram of the **learning process**:

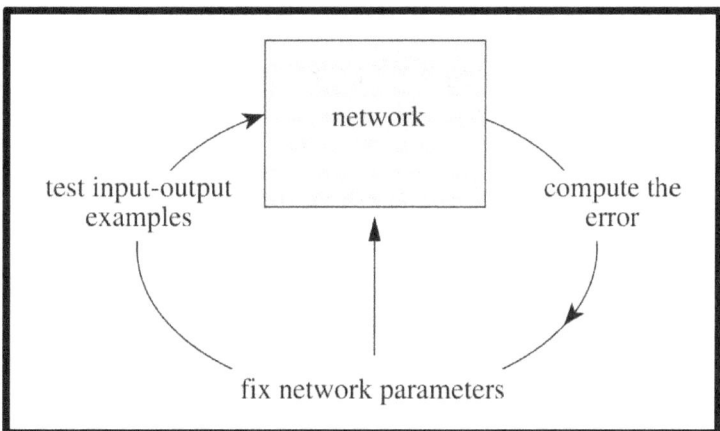

Figure 11.9: Learning in a Neural Network

A **perceptron** can be **trained on sample input-output sets** until it learns to compute the desired function. We use **perceptron learning algorithm** to implement the learning process. The algorithm is discussed in the following sections.

11.5.2 Perceptron Learning Algorithm:

Given: A classification problem with input vector (x_1, x_2, ..., x_n) & two output classes.

Compute: A set of weights (w_0, w_1, w_2, ..., w_n) that will cause a perceptron to fire whenever the input falls into the first output class.

1. Create a perceptron with n+1 input & n+1 weight, where the x_0 is always set to 1.

2. Initialize the weights (w_0, w_1, w_2, ..., w_n) to random real values.

3. Iterate through the training set, collecting all examples misclassified by the current set of weights.

4. If all examples are classified correctly, output the weights & quit.

5. Else, compute the vector sum S of the misclassified inputs. While calculating the sum S, add the following to S:

    5.1. Vector x if x is a vector for which the perceptron incorrectly fails to fire.
    5.2. Vector -x if x is a vector for which the perceptron incorrectly fires.

6. Modify the weights (w_0, w_1, w_2, ..., w_n) by adding the elements of vector S to them. Go to step 3.

11.5.3 Linear Separability:

Consider the pattern classification problem of the following figure:

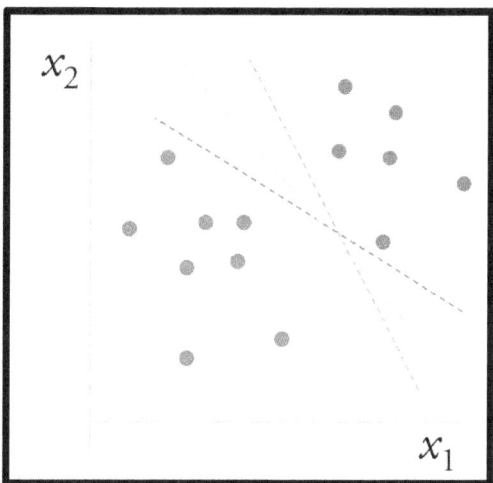

Figure 11.10: Linearly Separable Problem

The above figure contains two patterns: **red dots & blue dots**. We can draw a **straight line that separates both the class of patterns**. Thus, this classification problem is **linearly separable**. Given values for x_1 & x_2, we want to train a perceptron to **output 1 if the input belongs to blue dots & output 0 if the output belongs to red dots**.

First, let us have a look at what perceptron computes: Let **x be an input vector (x_1, x_2, ..., x_n)**. The **weighted summation function g(x) & the output function o(x)** can be defined as:

$$g(x) = \sum_{i=0}^{n}(x_i . w_i)$$

o(x) = 1 if g(x) > 0
       0 if g(x) < 0

In our case, we have **only two inputs (red dot & blue dot)**. Thus, in our case,

g(x) = w_0 + $x_1.w_1$ + $x_2.w_2$

If, **g(x) = 0**, the **perceptron won't be able to make a decision** & we'll get a **straight line**.
Let's get an **equation for a straight** line by substituting the **value of g(x) = 0**.

$$w_0 + x_1.w_1 + x_2.w_2 = 0$$
$$x_1.w_1 + x_2.w_2 = -w_0$$
$$x_1.w_1 = -w_0 - x_2.w_2$$
$$\boxed{x_1 = -\frac{w0}{w1} - \frac{w2}{w1}x_2}$$

We now get an **equation for a straight line**. The **position of the line completely depends on the weights w0, w1 & w2**. So, we can **adjust the value of weights** as per our requirements.

If an input vector lies on one side of the line, the perceptron will output 1, if the input lies on the other side of the line, perceptron will output 0. A **line that correctly separates the training instances corresponds to a perfect perceptron. Perceptron learning algorithm** can be applied on the above discussed problem to **determine the values of the weights**.

That's how a **linearly separable problem is solved** using a perceptron. Following is an example of **a problem that's linearly inseparable**:

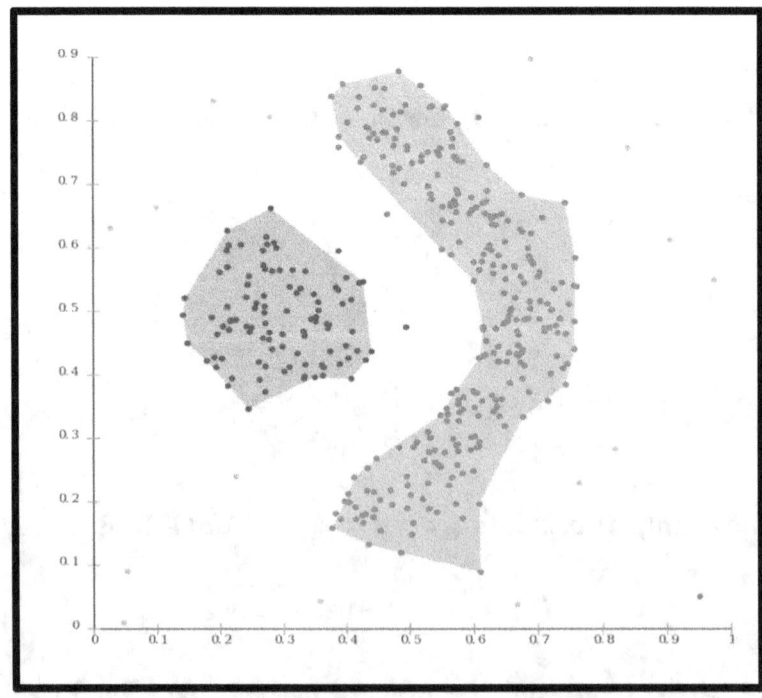

Figure 11.11: Linearly Inseparable Problem

11.5.4 Supervised and Unsupervised Learning:

Sr. No.	Supervised Learning	Unsupervised Learning
1	**Supervised learning** is a task of inferring a function from **labeled training data**.	**Unsupervised learning** is a task of trying to find hidden structure in **unlabeled training data**.
2	The training data consist of **pairs consisting of input values & desired output value**.	The training data contains **only input value, no output value**.
3	You use an algorithm to learn the mapping function from the input to the output.	Learning occurs on the basis of **structure of the training data**.
4	The **adjustment in the system are made on the basis of error signals** that are generated due to the difference in the desired output value & actual output value.	Since the examples given are unlabeled, there is **no error signal to evaluate a potential solution**.
5	It is a relatively simple process.	It is a complex process.
6	It represents the concept of humans teaching the computers.	It represents the concept of computers learning to teach themselves.
7	Most important example of supervised learning is **classification**.	Most important example of unsupervised learning is **clustering**.

11.6 Connectionist AI & Symbolic AI:

Sr. No.	Connectionist AI	Symbolic AI
1	An AI system that **mimics the functioning of human brain** (large number of inter-connected neurons).	An AI system based on **symbolic (human-readable) representations of problems**.
2	Connectionist representation of knowledge **proves to be learnable**.	Symbolic representation of knowledge is **not much learnable**.
3	Connectionist AI solves the problem but is **not able to effectively reason the solution**.	Symbolic AI have a **very good sense of reasoning** for the solved problem.
4	Connectionist representation of knowledge is **good in recognizing the shades of an entity having same meaning**.	Symbolic representation of knowledge is **not good in mapping the similarities** between like entities.
5	Connectionist AI has a **rich representation of knowledge**: For an instance, consider the phrases "mouth of bird" & "nose of bird". Connectionist representation of these phrases has no problem in mapping the similarities between mouth, nose & beak.	Connectionist AI has **difficulty matching the similarities** between like objects. This is because connectionist representation of an entity is given atomic label that bears no relation to any other entity.
6	**Flexible & robust** in nature due to the parallel processing of neurons.	**Not so flexible & robust**.
7	Common example: **Neural Networks**.	Common example: **Expert Systems**.

Introduction to PROLOG

12.1 Introduction to Prolog: Facts, Objects & Variables

PROLOG (Programming in Logic) is a programming language use for **symbolic & non-numeric computations**. Prolog is a **computer programming language** that is used for solving problems that involve **objects & the relationships between objects**.

Prolog should not be compared with object-oriented languages such as C++ & Java, because Prolog does a completely different job, and uses the word "object" in a completely different way. In Prolog, the word "object" does not refer to a data structure that can inherit variables & methods from a class, but it refers to things that we can represent using terms.

We first discuss **facts about objects**. The following things are important while representing a fact:

- The **names of all relationships & objects** must **begin with a lower-case letter**. For example, parent, tom, bob.

- The **relationship is written first & the objects are written separated by commas**, and the objects are **enclosed by a pair of round brackets**.

- **The dot character "." Must come at the end of a fact.**

The fact that **Tom is a parent of Bob** can be written in Prolog as:

parent (tom, bob).

Here, **Parent is the name of the relation** while **tom & bob are its objects**. When this **fact has been communicated to the Prolog** system, **Prolog can be asked some questions about this parent relation**. For an instance, the question: **"Is tom a parent of bob?"** can be communicated to Prolog by typing the following into the terminal:

?- parent (tom, bob).

Having found this as a **positive fact** in the program, Prolog will answer: **Yes**

Further query can be posted like:

?- parent (tom, kevin).

Prolog will answer: **No**

More interesting questions can also be asked. For example: **"Who is bob's parent?"**

?- parent (X, bob).

This time, the Prolog will not just answer Yes or No but **it will give us the value of X**.

X = tom

The *question*: *"who are tom's children?"* can be communicated as:

?- parent (tom, X).

The answer will be: **X = bob**

Our program can be asked an even ***broader question***: **"Who is a parent of whom?"**:

?- parent (X, Y).

The ***Prolog will answer all the available parent-child relationships***. In our case,

X = tom   Y = bob

Variables in Prolog:

Anything that starts with a capital letter is treated as a variable in Prolog. When Prolog uses a variable, the variable can be ***either instantiated or not instantiated***. ***Variable*** can be used to ***represent something that we can't name***. For example, we cannot name **"something that John likes"** as an object, so Prolog adopts a way of saying this. Instead of asking a question like:

?- likes (john, something that John likes).

Prolog lets us use variables, like this:

?- likes (john, X).

12.2 Conjunctions in Prolog (Backward Chaining):

Suppose we wish to answer *questions about more complicated relationships* such as, *"Do John and Mary like each other?"* One way to do this would be *first to ask if John likes Mary, and if Prolog tells us yes, then we ask if Mary likes John*. So, this problem consists of *two separate goals* that the Prolog system must try to satisfy. We represent this by *putting a comma between the goals*:

?- likes (john, mary), likes (mary, john).

The comma is pronounced *"and"*, & it serves to *separate any number of different goals* that have to be satisfied in order to answer a question.

Now, let us consider an *example to understand the backward chaining* that Prolog uses to *evaluate conjunctions*. Consider that we have the following *facts in our database*:

likes (mary, chocolate).
likes (mary, wine).
likes (john, wine).
likes (john, mary).

Now let us consider this *question:* "Is anything that's liked by Mary also liked by John?" This question can be represented as conjunction in the following manner:

?- likes(mary, X) , likes(john, X).

- The *database is searched for the first goal*. As the second argument (X) is not instantiated, it may take any value in future. The first fact in our database that matches the goal is *likes (mary, chocolate)*. So, now *X is instantiated to chocolate* everywhere in the question where X appears. *Prolog marks the place in the database* where it found the fact, so it can return to this point in case it needs to re-satisfy the goal.

- Now, the *database is searched for likes (john, chocolate)*. This is because the *next goal is likes (john, X), & X currently stands for chocolate*. As you can see, *no such fact exists, so the goal fails*.

- Now **when a goal fails, we must try to re-satisfy the previous goal**, so *Prolog attempts to re-satisfy likes (mary, X)*, but this time *starting from the point that was marked in the database while satisfying the goal previously*.

- The *marked place is likes (mary, chocolate)*, so *Prolog begins searching from that fact*. Because *we have not reached the end of the database yet, we have not exhausted the possibilities of what Mary likes*, and the *next satisfying fact is likes (mary, wine)*. The variable *X is now instantiated to wine, & Prolog marks the place* in case it must re-satisfy what mary likes.

- *Prolog now tries the second goal*, searching this time for *likes (john, wine)*. Prolog is *not trying to re-satisfy this goal, it is entering the goal again* so it must *start searching from the beginning of the database*. After not too much searching, *the matching fact is found, & Prolog notifies you*. Since this goal was satisfied, *Prolog also marks its place in the database*, in case you want to re-satisfy the goal.

- At this point, *both goals have been satisfied*. Variable *X stands for the name "wine"*. The *first goal has a place-marker* in the database at the fact likes (mary, wine), & the *second goal has a place-marker* in the database at the fact likes (john, wine).

As soon as Prolog finds one answer, it stops & waits for further instructions. If we press `;` `↵` , Prolog will search for more things that both John & Mary like, starting from the place-markers left behind.

This is how *Prolog uses **Backward chaining** to prove or answer any given goal*.

12.3 List Manipulation in Prolog:

A *list is a sequence of any number of items*, such as winter, tennis, tom, skiing. Such a list can be *written in Prolog as*:

[winter, tennis, tom, skiing]

A *list is either empty or non-empty. If it is empty*, it is **simple written** as an atom, []. *If it is non-empty*, it can be viewed as a **collection of two things**:

- *Head:* the *first item* of the list.
- *Tail:* the *remaining part* of the list.

For the example discussed above, **head is 'winter' & the tail is [tennis, tom, skiing]**. Head can be any Prolog object such as a variable. The **tail has to be a list**. The **head & tail are then combined into a structure** by a special function. The choice of this function depends on the Prolog implementation; we will assume here that it is the dot:

.(Head, Tail)

Since **Tail is also a list, it is either empty or it has its own head & tail**. Therefore, our example list is then represented as the term:

.(winter, .(tennis, .(tom, .(skiing, []))))

However, when such lists are output to a program, they are **automatically converted to their neater form**. So, the following conversion in Prolog is possible:

?- List1 = [a, b, c],
List2 = .(a, .(b, .(c, []))).
List1 = [a, b, c]
List2 = [a, b, c]

In Prolog, the **list can be declared in the following ways**:

- [Item1, Item2, ...]

- [Head | Tail]

12.3.1 Membership in a List:

Let us implement the *membership relation* as:

$$member (X, L)$$

where *X is an object & L is a list*. The *goal member (X, L) is true if X occurs in L*. For example,

$$member (b, [a, b, c]) \text{ is TRUE.}$$

$$member (b, [a, [b, c]]) \text{ is NOT TRUE}$$

$$member ([b, c], [a, [b, c]]) \text{ is TRUE}$$

The *program for the membership relation* can be based on the following observation:

X is a member of L if,

- Either *X is the head of L*,
- Or *X is a member of the tail of L*.

12.3.2 Concatenation of Lists:

For concatenating multiple lists, we will define the **concatenation relation:**

$$conc\ (L1,\ L2,\ L3)$$

Here **L1 & L2 are two lists, & L3 is their concatenation.** For example,

$$conc\ ([a,\ b],\ [c,\ d],\ [a,\ b,\ c,\ d])\ is\ true$$
$$conc\ ([a,\ b],\ [c,\ d],\ [a,\ b,\ a,\ c,\ d])\ is\ false$$

In the **definition of conc** we will have **two cases**, depending on the first argument, L1:

1. If the **first argument is the empty list** then the **second & the third arguments must be the same list** (call it L). this is expressed by the following Prolog fact:

$$conc\ ([],\ L,\ L).$$

2. If the **first argument of conc is a non-empty list** then **it has a head & a tail** and must look like this:

$$[X\ |\ L1]$$

The **result of the concatenation is the list $[X\ |\ L3]$** where **L3 is the concatenation of L1 & L2.** In prolog this is written as:

$$conc\ ([X\ |\ L1],\ L2,\ [X\ |\ L3])\ :-\ conc\ (L1,\ L2,L3).$$

This program can now be used for concatenating given lists, for example:

$$?-\ conc\ ([a,\ b,\ c],\ [1,\ 2,\ 3],\ L).$$
$$L = [a,\ b,\ c,\ 1,\ 2,\ 3]$$

$$?-\ conc\ ([a,\ [b,\ c],\ d],\ [a,\ [],\ b],\ L).$$
$$L = [a,\ [b,\ c],\ d,\ a,\ [],\ b]$$

The following figure illustrates the **concatenation of $[X\ |\ L1]$ & some list L2:**

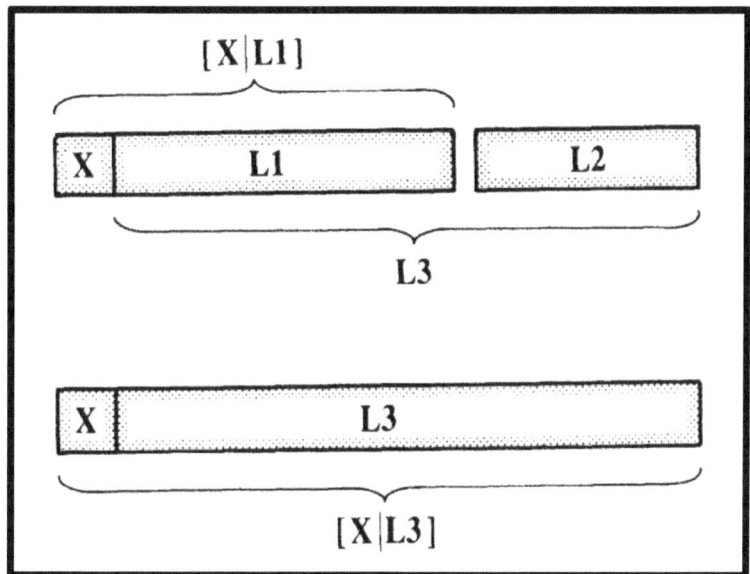

Figure 12.1: List Concatenation in Prolog

We can also **use conc program in the reverse direction for decomposing a given list into two lists**, as follows:

$$?- conc\ (L1,\ L2,\ [a,\ b,\ c]).$$

$$L1 = []$$
$$L2 = [a,\ b,\ c];$$

$$L1 = [a]$$
$$L2 = [b,\ c];$$

$$L1 = [a,\ b]$$
$$L2 = [c];$$

$$L1 = [a,\ b,\ c]$$
$$L2 = [];$$

no

12.3.3 Adding & Deleting from a List:

Adding to a List:

To *add an item to a list*, it is easiest to *put the new item in front of the list* so that *it becomes the new head*. If *X is the new item* & the *list to which X is added is L* then the *resulting list is simply*:

$$[X \mid L]$$

We actually need no procedure for adding a new element in front of the list. Nevertheless, if we want to define such a procedure, it can be written as the fact:

$$\text{add } (X, L, [X \mid L]).$$

Deleting from a List:

Deleting an item, X, from a list, L, can be programmed as a relation

$$\text{del } (X, L, L1)$$

where *L1 is equal to the list L with the item X removed*. The "del" *relation* can be defined similarly to the membership relation. we have **two cases**:

1. If *X is the head of the list* then the *result after the deletion is the tail of the list.*

$$\text{del } (X, [X \mid Tail], Tail).$$

2. If *X is in the tail* then it is deleted from there.

$$\text{del } (X, [Y \mid Tail], [Y \mid Tail]) :- \text{del } (X, Tail, Tail).$$

If there are *several occurrences of X* in the list then each alternative execution of *del will only delete one of them*. For example:

$$?- \text{del } (a, [a, b, a, a], L).$$

$$L = [b, a, a];$$

L = [a, b, a];
L = [a, b, a];
no

del can also be used in the reverse direction, to ***add an item to a list by inserting the new item anywhere in the list***. For example, if we want to insert 'a' at any place in the list [1, 2, 3] then we can do this by asking the question: ***"what is L such that after deleting 'a' from L we obtain [1, 2, 3] ?"***

?- del (a, L, [1, 2, 3]).
L = [a, 1, 2, 3];
L = [1, a, 2, 3];
L = [1, 2, a, 3];
L = [1, 2, 3, a];
no

12.3.4 Sub-List:

The **sublist relation** has **two arguments**, a list L & a list S such that S occurs within L as its sub-list. So,

sublist ([c, d, e], [a, b, c, d, e, f]) is TRUE
sublist ([c, e], [a, b, c, d, e, f]) is FALSE

The **Prolog program for sublist** can be based on the following facts:

S is a sublist of L if:

1. L can be decomposed into two lists, L1 & L2
2. L2 can be decomposed into two lists, S & some L3.

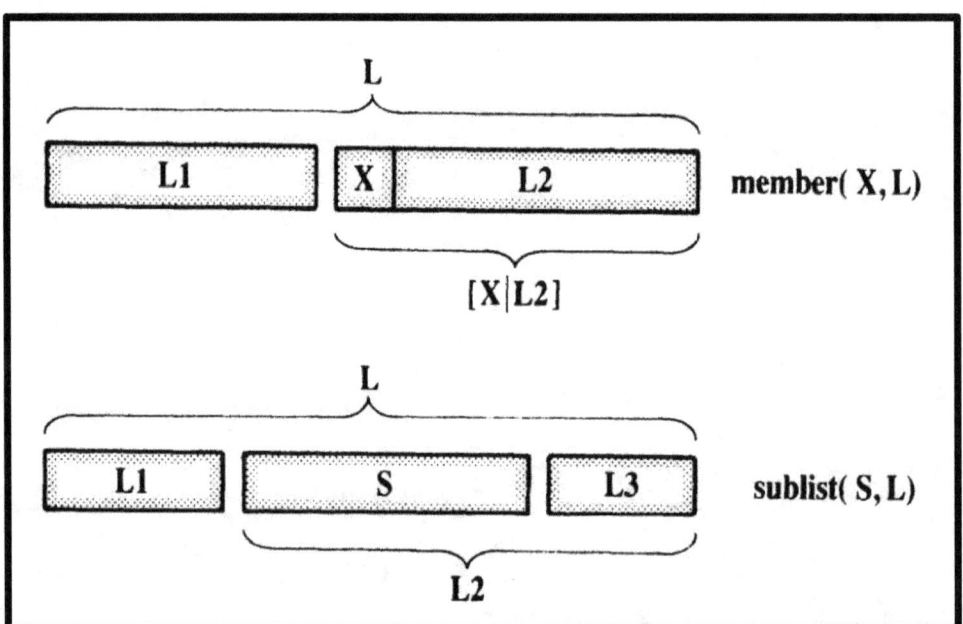

Figure 12.2: Membership & Sublist in Prolog Lists

12.4 Cut, Fail & Repeat Predicates in Prolog:

12.4.1 Cut:

The **cut predicate** in Prolog, written as '**!**', is a **goal that always succeeds** but **doesn't allow backtracking.** It is used to **prevent unwanted backtracking**, for example, to **prevent multiple solutions from being found by Prolog.**

Let us discuss an example. Consider that we have the following **facts in our database:**

likes (mary, chocolate).

likes (mary, wine).

likes (john, wine).

likes (john, mary).

Now consider the following **query & it's output:**

?- likes(mary, X) , likes(john, X).

X = wine;
false

Backtracking is allowed here. X is first bound to chocolate but john doesn't like chocolate, so the **second goal fails. Backtracking occurs & X is now bound to wine**, john likes wine & the **second goal succeeds. The value of X is wine.**

Now consider the following **query that contains cut predicate:**

?- likes(mary, X) , !, likes(john, X).

false

This time, *X is initially bound to chocolate* & then *cut goal is executed.* Then, second goal is executed. John doesn't like chocolate, so the **second goal fails. Backtracking is not allowed here due to the cut predicate**, so the **whole query fails.**

Another **example for cut predicate** is given as follows:

```
dountilstop :-
  repeat,
  read(X),
  (X = stop, !
  ;
   process(X), fail
  ).
```

In this case, the **code reads data, one term at a time, from the current input stream.** The **call to fail is there to force backtracking.** The **call to repeat is there to force the code to endlessly repeat** until something terminates the backtracking. This **"something"** is the **"cut" predicate** after **X = stop**. If the **term read is the atom "stop"**, the goal "X = stop" succeeds, the cut is executed, and the rule terminates.

12.4.2 Fail:

Fail is a **built-in predicate in Prolog & has no arguments**. As the name suggests, **this predicate always fails**. It is **used for forcing backtracking** & for various other purposes.

Consider the following **example for the fail predicate:**

```
dountilstop :-
  repeat,
  read(X),
  (X = stop, !
   ;
   process(X), fail
  ).
```

In this case, the **code reads data, one term at a time, from the current input stream**. The **call to fail is there to force backtracking**. The **call to repeat is there to force the code to endlessly repeat** until something terminates the backtracking. This **"something"** is the **"cut" predicate** after **X = stop**. If the **term read is the atom "stop"**, the **goal "X = stop" succeeds**, the **cut is executed, and the rule terminates**.

12.4.3 Repeat:

Repeat is the **built-in predicate** which behaves as if defined as follows:

> repeat.
> repeat :- repeat.

repeat succeeds when first called, due to the first predicate. If the Prolog interpreter subsequently backtracks, the second clause (repeat :- repeat.) is tried. This initiates a new call to repeat which succeeds via the first predicate, and so on. This predicate is **used to make the code infinitely repeat** until something terminates it.

Consider the following **example for the repeat predicate:**

```
dountilstop :-
  repeat,
  read(X),
  (X = stop, !
  ;
   process(X), fail
  ).
```

In this case, the **code reads data, one term at a time, from the current input stream.** The **call to fail is there to force backtracking.** The **call to repeat is there to force the code to endlessly repeat** until something terminates the backtracking. This **"something"** is the **"cut" predicate** after $X = stop$. If the **term read is the atom "stop"**, the **goal "$X = stop$" succeeds**, the **cut is executed, and the rule terminates.**

12.5 Terminologies in Prolog:

1. **_Fact / Predicate_**: A fact or a predicate asserts some property of an object, or relation between two or more objects. Each predicate has a name, and zero or more arguments. For example:

   parent (jane, alan).

   The above fact can be read as "Jane is the parent of Alan." The predicate name is 'parent' & the arguments are 'jane' & 'alan'.

2. **_Rule_**: A rule allows us to infer that a relationship holds true based on the specified preconditions. For example:

   parent (X, Y) :- mother (X, Y).

   The above rule specifies that "Person X is the parent of person Y **if** X is Y's mother."

3. **_Clause_**: A clause can either be a fact / predicate or it can be a rule. If the clause is a fact, it won't have a body because facts are always true. If the clause is a rule, it will have both a head & a body. For example:

   ```
   mother(jane,alan).           = Fact
   parent(P1,P2):- mother(P1,P2).   = Rule
           ↑              ↑
          head           body
   ```

4. **_Domain_**: Domain of a particular variable can be defined by the values that can be assigned to that variable.
5. **_Goal_**: A goal is a Prolog term that denotes some fact / predicate & its arguments. The body of a rule is a Prolog goal. The purpose of submitting a goal is to find

out whether the statement represented by the goal is true according to the knowledge database.

6. **_Cut_**: The cut predicate in Prolog, written as '!', is a goal that always succeeds but doesn't allow backtracking. It is used to prevent unwanted backtracking, for example, to prevent multiple solutions from being found by Prolog.

7. **_Fail_**: Fail is a built-in predicate in Prolog & has no arguments. As the name suggests, this predicate always fails. It is used for forcing backtracking and for various other purposes.

8. **_Repeat_**: Repeat is the built-in predicate which behaves as if defined as follows:

repeat.
repeat :- repeat.

repeat succeeds when first called, due to the first predicate. If the Prolog interpreter subsequently backtracks, the second clause (repeat :- repeat.) is tried. This initiates a new call to repeat which succeeds via the first predicate, and so on.

9. **_Inference Engine_**: Inference engine in Prolog uses backward chaining & is used to prove or disprove the specified predicates. Prolog rules are used for the knowledge representation, and the Prolog inference engine is used to derive conclusions. Inference engines can also be used to partially implement some expert systems.

12.6 Prolog Programs:

A Prolog program is a set of predicates.

12.6.1 Example 1:

Prolog program to find sum of all the numbers of a list.

Program:

list_sum ([ ], 0).

list_sum ([Head | Tail], Sum) :-

    list_sum (Tail, TempSum),
    Sum is Head + TempSum.

Query:

list_sum ([-2, 6], Sum).

Result:

Sum = 4

12.6.2 Example 2:

Prolog program to find maximum number from a list.

Program:

list_max ([P | T], Max) :- list_max (T, P, Max).

list_max ([ ], P, P).

list_max ([H | T], P, Max) :-
  (
    H > P
  -> list_max (T, H, Max)
  ; list_max (T, P, Max)
).

Query:

list_max ([1, 2, 3, 4, 5, 6, 86], Max).

Result:

Max = 86

12.6.3 Example 3:

Prolog program to find the factorial of a number.

Program:

fact (0, Answer):- Answer is 1.

fact (X, Answer):-

> Temp is X-1,
> fact (Temp, S),
> Answer is S*X.

Query:

fact (5, Factorial).

Result:

Factorial = 120

12.6.4 Example 4:

Write a Prolog program for finding a set, which is result of the intersection of the two given sets.

Hint:
Goal: intersect ([1, 2, 3], [2, 3, 4], A)
     A = [2, 3]

Goal: intersect ([d, f, g], [a, b, c], X)
X = []

Program:

intersection (_ , [ ] , [ ]) :- !.

intersection ([ ] , _ , [ ]) :- !.

intersection ([H1 | T1] , L2 , [H1 | L]) :-

    member (H1 , L2),
    intersection (T1 , L2 , L) , !.

intersection ([_ | T1] , L2 , L) :-

    intersection (T1 , L2 , L).

Query:

intersection ([a , b , c] , [c] , L).

Result:

L = [c]

12.6.5 Example 5:

Write a Prolog program to merge two sequentially ordered (ascending) lists into one ordered list.

Hint:

Goal: merge ([1, 3, 5, 7], [0, 2, 4, 6], L)
L = [0, 1, 2, 3, 4, 5, 6, 7]

Goal: merge ([a, c], [b, d], [a, b, c, d])
Yes

Program:

merge ([ ], [ ], [ ]).

merge ([X], [ ], [X]).

merge ([ ], [Y], [Y]).

merge ([X | List1], [Y | List2], [X | List]) :-

    X < Y, !, merge (List1, [Y | List2], List), !.

merge ([X | List1], [Y | List2], [Y | List]) :-

    merge ([X | List1], List2, List), !.

Query:

merge ([a , b , c] , [c] , L).

Result:

L = [a, b, c, c]

12.6.6 Example 6:

Write a Prolog program to find the last element of a list.

Program:

find_last (L, Ans) :- last (L, Ans).

Query:

find_last ([a , b , c], Answer).

Result:

Answer = c

12.6.7 Example 7:

Write a Prolog program to find the number of elements of a list.

Program:

find_count (L, Ans) :- length (L, Ans).

Query:

find_count ([a , b , c], Answer).

Result:

Answer = 3

12.6.8   Example 8:

Write a Prolog program to reverse a list.

Program:

find_reverse (L, Ans) :- reverse (L, Ans).

Query:

find_reverse ([a , b , c], Answer).

Result:

Answer = [c, b, a]

12.6.9 Example 9:

Write a Prolog program to check if list is a palindrome.

Program:

```
is_palindrome ( L ) :- reverse ( L, RL ), equals ( L, RL ).

equals ( A, B ):-
   A = B
   ->  write ( ' list is palindrome! ' )
   ;   write ( ' list is not palindrome! ' ).
```

Query:

```
is_palindrome ( [ a , b , c ] ).
```

Result:

list is not palindrome!

12.6.10 Example 10:

Prolog program to find minimum number from a list.

Program:

list_min ([P | T], Min) :- list_min (T, P, Min).

list_min ([ ], P, P).

list_min ([H | T], P, Min) :-
  (
    H < P
  -> list_ min (T, H, Min)
  ; list_ min (T, P, Min)
).

Query:

list_min ([1, 2, 3, 4, 5, 6, 86], Min).

Result:

Min = 1

12.6.11 Example 11:

Prolog program to check if a number is present in the list.

Program:

findnum (X, [X | _]):-

    write (" **Number Is Found** "), !.

findnum (X, [_ | Tail]) :-

    findnum (X, Tail).

Query:

findnum (2, [1, 2, 3]).

Result:

Number is found
true

12.6.12   Example 12:

Prolog program to print Fibonacci series for n terms.

Program:

fib (0) :- write (' number of elements can not be 0 '), !.

fib (1) :- write (' 0 '), !.

fib (N) :-
   Count is 2,
   write (' 0, 1 '),
   printdata (N, Count, 0, 1).

printdata (N, Count, N1, N2):-

   Count < N   ->

   Data is N1 + N2,
   write (', '),
   write (Data),
   printdata (N, Count + 1, N2, Data)   ;

   !.

Query:

fib (7).

Result:

0, 1, 1, 2, 3, 5, 8

www.ingramcontent.com/pod-product-compliance
Lightning Source LLC
Chambersburg PA
CBHW082104220526
45472CB00009B/2043